FROM THE HEART

Poems by John Core

Trafford rev. 02/06/2024

 www.trafford.com

North America & international
toll-free: 844-688-6899 (USA & Canada)
fax: 812 355 4082

The poems are printed in the order in which they
were written over a period of 18 months.
However, the table of contents is organized
on a theme basis for those of you who
prefer a roadmap.

The collection is dedicated to Donna.
Thanks to Jo-Anne Aylard for encouraging
me to write.

Enjoy these poems from my heart.

John Core

TABLE OF CONTENTS

EMERGING EMOTION

SELF DISCOVERY

HUMAN CONNECTION

FAMILY

HOME ON THE FARM

SURGERY

WAR AND POVERTY

POTPOURRI

TRANSITION

Birth and death mark the beginning and end.
Transitions fill the void between.
One phase to another, one experience to another.
The constant ebb and flow of life
New friends, old friends, lifetime friends
Happiness, sadness, love and bitterness
Transitions all, the essence of life.

The river of life flows on.
Unexpected obstacles appear
Held back, the current slows, the swirling begins
Back and forth, up and down
Searching for the way to move on
The life force feels spent, the future unclear.

An emotional cloudburst floods your being
Life's energy is renewed
The dam is breached
Transition resumes
Life moves on from beginning to end.

THE PASSAGE

I've felt the freedom of a small place
A place that embraced and held me secure
A place where I could feel love
A place where my future was the stuff of dreams
Not my dreams but the dreams of others
The time for a new world had come
Some irresistible force pushed me on

It was a difficult passage
I emerge into a bright cold place
I no longer float free
I am held and supported by some alien being
The breath of life enters my body
I welcome it with a cry of anguish and then delight
Sound surrounds me
I am placed in my mother's arms
I feel embraced once again by love
I have arrived!

SILENCE INVADES

The farm has changed
No cows, no calves, no routine
Quiet, cold and forlorn
Each generation brought growth until today
Today brought emptiness
The barn is silent; the stalls stand vacant
Frozen in a moment of time.
The view from the kitchen window stays the same
The lives of those who live within have shifted
The chores no longer beckon before the sun rises
The late night calvings no longer intrude
The frantic activity has slowed and on a winter day has stopped
After 150 toil filled years the barn stands empty
All my life it has been part of home
Home has changed
Oh how the silence rings!

HELD IN LOVE

My mother's arms surround me with love
They hold and shelter me from the outside world
I feel whole and complete within them
My world is safe and secure.

Her arms pick me up when I awake
They lay me down when it's time for sleep
I dream soundly knowing those arms await me
When hunger calls,
Her hands guide my hungry mouth to her full breast
They cradle my head as I suckle
Her fingers explore every part of me.
From the top of my head to the tips of my toes
Her touch soothes and comforts me.
Ripples of tenderness caress me.

I am in the arms of love.

BEYOND THE LIMITS

Life has many boundaries
Whose lines we dare not cross.
Should my world have such fences,
Forbidden limits I must not pass?
Are there experiences I need not feel?
Are there people not to know?
Are there sunrises not to see
Or sunsets beyond my view?
I think not but others do!

Fear and uncertainty create these boundaries.
Without boundaries the end is never reached
Without an end there is no comfort
For those of us who comfort seeks.

Ignore the boundaries!
Let me fly
On a never ending quest
To find the next fulfilling place
To meet my needs and give me peace
Out beyond the limits.

THE SOUNDS WITHIN

Years ago,
On a strong foundation supported by rough-hewn logs,
The Murphys built me as their home.
Lofty trees have shaded me,
Flower beds have graced me.
Those who dwelled within have lived their lives
From birth to death.

In between, my walls have felt the sounds of life and love
... the warming flow of laughter
... the sadness of unfilled dreams
... the fury and hurt of anger spent
... the calmness of forgiveness given
... the loud congratulations of success
... the strength for failures felt

Now the future beckons.
Though I know not who may next dwell herein,
Their sounds will feel the same.

THE SENTINEL

The aged oak
A stalwart sentinel
Guarding part of nature.
Its' leaves rustle gently in the summer breeze
Amid scattered barren broken branches
(the consequence of passing storms).
Tall and lonely it seems.....

Listen carefully
The sounds of songbirds caress its stature
The startled cries of blackbirds rise
The soothing calls of doves lament the passing day
A cacophony of sound and sight
A home for nature's flying things
A haven on the sparse landscape
A symbol of life and majesty.

ANTICIPATION

Spring beckons!
The landscape stands muted, stark against the horizon
Waiting for a tinge of colour to appear.
The maples yearn for their shroud of richness
To feed the flow of new life and growth.
The grass is preparing to burst through its mask of death
Seeking nourishing rays of sunshine.
Crocuses are tentatively feeling the earth
Searching out the warmth they seek.
Nature has withstood the ravishes of cold
Patiently holding its breath for the warm winds to blow.
The animals are restless as winter lingers.
Food is scarce in the brown reserves.
Pond waters sigh with the promise of new freedom.
The bonds of ice are gone,
Sunrays shimmer, stirring awake the depths.
Whispers of spring caress the woodlots, fields, and streams.

Anticipation builds!
New life takes time to form.
Green will soon burst through
Birthing a wave of joy to flood the landscape.

INDEPENDENCE

Off our children go to find their world
Down the path to where, one wonders.
We've helped build their lives
And now must watch them leave
To test their values and pursue their hopes
Feel the failures and search themselves.
It's hard to let them leave our care
Despite the knowledge they must go.
Independence must be felt
Without such growth they founder.

To build their hopes and not let them leave
May feed us but not their lives.
Too often parental bonds confine
Beyond the years that nature calls.
There is a time to hold on tight
But love means we must search deep within ourselves
Find the strength to do what's right.
Open the door and ease them out
Our job is done, their world awaits.

MY SONG OF LIFE

Within the crowded channels of my mind
My unfinished song of life lies waiting
For new sounds and words to add.
Did I compose this song
Or did others write the melody
That I took to be my own?
Upon close scrutiny it would appear
There are only muted feelings in the words.
Little passion, little laughter.
It seems not enough!
Is there some more basic inner tune
To be my song of life?

I search deep
I find it waiting to be heard
I play it often
I play it loud
I let it fill my heart
I share it with others and let them know
Their song awaits them too.

ADVENTURE CALLS

A simple laneway through the farm,
For my childhood eyes, became
The road I walked
To explore the world.

My first footsteps upon this lane
Were tenuous, small and proud.
My mother's hand held mine tight
The unknown stretched before us.

Soon her hand was left behind
My growing legs were long
I ventured forth to find my way
Alone but feeling strong

I cast my eyes forward
Along the narrow lane
The corn cast deep shadows
I hesitate

I took a big breath
Focused all my thoughts
That day I made the first hill
Before my fears took hold

The next day I wait till noon
The pathway was shining bright
No shadows impede my progress
The third hill was in sight

Now the path is straight and level
Perhaps a curve or two
Not a hill
To block the view

My steps grow longer
With each passing year
Occasionally they shorten
The next child takes my hand

Soon that clasp is broken
Their stride lengthens
Two now walk where one has passed
Their independence strengthens

A simple lane so it seemed
To those who did not walk it
But life's adventure just begun
For those who trod upon it

FOOTSTEPS

The dark patterns of shadows merge
Winter dusk melts into darkness.
The rising moon casts a blanket of light
Across the earth bound bed of snow.
Trees and shrubs stark against the spread of white.
Melted footsteps stretch off across the meadow
—- not a solitary path —-
Rather a journey together of father and child.
Across the frozen landscape they have wandered.
The father's footsteps firm and deep
The steps beside are two for one.
The paths taken do not diverge
Bound together by hands held tight.

A DAUGHTER'S LOVE

He was my father, small and proud
He loved me deeply and I in turn
He was my family and let me know
They'd chosen me and I was special

My mother was gone much too early
Her love had filled my soul
My father moved to fill the space
His unspoken words gave me strength

He was proud of me and what I was
My children filled his heart with joy
He respected my life and gave me space
He let me know he was always there

As he grew old he became
Not the man I'd known
Gone his very nature
Hidden in the cloud of time

The spirit I loved still dwelled within
Not marred by time or features changed
At times the spirit soared so high
Brief glimpses returned

It was now my turn to care and nurture
Fill the void that age had brought
His lifelong love was now returned
With willing heart and hands

As the end drew near my unwept tears appeared
My memories of past became the fuel
That allowed me to let him know
I was safe and he could go

TAKE OFF AND FLY

High above me seven contrails,
Reflected by the rays of the setting sun,
Cleave the clear blue sky.

The planes and those within are moving on.
The marks they leave are where they've been.
They had set their course and ventured forth.
Their destination beckons.

Looking back I see my life
Stretched out to where I've been.
Each second ticking marked a passing.
Each thought I've had became the past.

Each day I have a flight path.
Decisions to make along the way.
My world awaits!
I take off and fly
I think not about the landing
The journey is the pleasure
I soar high and feel the light
My spirit seeks new height.

SWIRLING

Round, round, round they go
The thoughts, the images, the feelings
They bounce from one another
They collide, merge and imbed themselves

"What if? what if? what if?" they shout
Never content to be
Are other peoples' minds like this?
Never ending processing

Searching, searching, searching
Never finding peace
Make the swirling stop
Drown those useless thoughts

Focus on the present
Think not about tomorrow
Life is unpredictable
Impossible to make it so

Let pleasant thoughts flood your brain
Crowd out the spacey whirling
This isn't always easy
The chatter isn't dead

Accept for now the struggle
Serenity lies ahead.

SOUND BREAKS THROUGH

Morning light brightens the room
Thoughts rush through my head
Bits of dreams, fragments of past
The "what ifs" of today
Tumbling round and round

Out beyond my window
A mournful whistle calls
Through my jumbled thoughts
I hear the train approaching

The swirling thoughts are set aside
A simple sound has done it
A momentary calmness settles
An image fills the void

My thoughts turn to action
The past is energy spent
It's time to change the focus
Calm my racing thoughts

Life is not a jungle
Of unfilled thoughts and dreams
Rather it's like a meadow
Stretching on forever
With no limit to what I can do.

THE PASSING

The quiet seems unbroken
As friends and family gather.
The silent words of sorrow
Assail my broken heart.
The sight of falling tears
Brings forth the same from me.
The touch of those who mourn
Enforce the bonds we feel.
A loved one lost to passing time
Brings those who grieve together
To feel the loss and gather strength
For life among the living.

LATER

I remember all the joyful times.
The times we spent together.
The love of family firm and strong,
Friendship truly shared.
Trust and honour were for him
Virtues to pursue.
The sorrow and pain of loss just felt
Mingles with those memories.
The sounds of life grow louder
Muffled sounds of laughter rise
As all of those within that room
Celebrate the life just lived.

STRENGTH AGAINST THE STORM

The windows vibrate as the walls hold back
the howling winter storm.
Snow is hurled horizontally across the frozen fields.
Above the swirling white wall can be seen
the tops of wind bent trees,
The hidden bare branches hum with sound.
Power lines dance between the spindle poles.
Drifts come and go as direction shifts.
Momentarily the wind dies,
cars appear intermittently down the snow buried roads.
The landscape reappears,
soon to be hidden once again,
by another burst of driven snow.
Isolated by this power of nature,
we stay huddled warm and close.
Through winter storms and summer heat,
our refuge stands secure.

The storm passes.
The wind now gently chills the eaves.
The snow-covered fields are calm.
The sparrows appear to search for winter food.
The exuberant voices of children cleave the silence.
Our refuge rests
To sustain its strength
To withstand the next challenge of wind and storm.

OUR SPIRIT

What is the thing that drives us?
So the question goes
Spirit is the answer some may say

It is the boundless energy
To fuel the steps we take
Along our lifelong journey

It is the hidden passion
That makes us want to find
A place to rest and feel at home

It is the fervent yearning
To search and find a love
To share our heart and joy

It is the untapped strength
To find some hidden meaning
When all we have is spent

It calls to us quite loudly
To become what we desire
Despite what others wish

Our spirit is our life force
Waiting patiently
For us to call it forth

THE NEXT STEP

I want to find the balance
of calm within while seeking challenge out beyond.
I want to feel a wholeness in all I feel and do.
My spirit feels the inner battle.
Can I become a whole?
A whole that every person seeks but few are brave enough to find.
A whole that holds the promise for peace to flood my soul.
Is that the search I'm on?
Is that the reason for this tension that grips my every breath?
Can I breathe deep and let it go?
Touch base within,
find one track to send my thoughts thundering along,
no destination firm in mind.
Is that the spirit that I seek?
A freedom not to think!

To feel each gentle murmur of voices held within,
To hear the unspoken words of others,
To see their hidden yearnings,
To feel the force of life's free flow,
To write about it all.
Perhaps, the secret to this quest
Is to unlock the bonds that hold emotions deep within.
Share my thoughts with others,
Open up my inner self,
Expose it to the world.

WANDERING IS DONE

Through life's experience we wander
No map to guide our path
No destination within our grasp.
"Where will our spirit take us?"
Ask those who want to feel secure in every step they take.
There is no set direction,
Only choices along the way.

Heed the voice within you
No matter how faint the whisper.
Ignore the distractions
Your inner self is showing you the way.
Be not afraid, it won't be wrong
The voice of self knows what you need.
Put down your foot and take that path
The wandering is done.

PASSING THOUGHT

We hold our feelings very tight
Shrouded within the veil of night.
Keeping them from the probing light
That would unmask our inner fright
Of being in a quiet place
Alone in our own space.

HOSTAGE

From the dark caves of my mind
Random thoughts emerge like startled bats
To fill the empty time.
They tumble and twist
Seeking some common thread
To create sense among the jumbled chaos.
Energy builds from colliding thoughts.
Unbidden it seeps through my being.
Held in, it gathers just below the surface
Waiting impatiently to burst forth.
Unable to escape it burrows deeper
Tightening its hold around my inner parts.
Tension grips my entirety,
I'm hostage to my inner thoughts.
I struggle to loosen the bonds
That keep me from moving on.

SHROUD OF FEAR

Our emotions are seldom seen by those around us.
They are held back in the shadows of our minds,
Hidden by a shroud of fear.
We dare not let others see our private selves.
Extremes of passion are not seen as strengths
In a culture where masks of blandness rule.
How much richer would our lives be
If the shrouds were torn, the masks removed
To set our feelings free.

WHAT LINGERS ON

This is what a life should be!

A quiet acknowledgement of passing time
No regrets or undreamed dreams
The quiet repose of a peaceful spirit
The warm flow of a deep breath
A heart filled each day to bursting
The bubbles of a child's laughter
The safety of your parents' arms
Shimmering memories of their love
The loud joy of times around the kitchen table
The wonder of your first true love
The perfection of your newborn daughters' smooth skin

A life thus filled will not the seconds mark
The details of daily living fade
The intellectual achievements will be surpassed
What lingers on are memories
That touched our inner self.

THE WINDS OF MEMORY

Memories sweep through my being
Like winds through a stalwart maple.
Some feel like the gentle breezes of summer
Sending a warm caressing pleasure
Cascading through my senses
Filling my spirit with tranquillity.
Some are like the roaring winds of a summer storm
Whipping my senses to and fro
Tearing at my very centre
Allowing raw emotion to spill forth
From broken bits unable to withstand the turmoil.
Some are like the frigid sting of a northern wind
During the dark days of winter
Waking me from complacency
Reminding me of how brittle my sense of self has become.
Some are like the fresh smelling wafts of spring
Tickling my thoughts with past fancies
Filling my heart with yearnings for new things
Making me dig deep to find the source of my pleasure
Stirring new growth in what I can be.
At times the memories are silent
I live in the moment and feel at ease
Waiting for the next wind to blow.

RULES

Many children learn the rules
That haunt their adult life.
Suppress your inner self.
Do what others want.
Create that cool calm look
That dissuades all from looking deeper.
Build defences around your being
To protect you from the storms.
Let not emotions rule your actions
Rationale and reason are all that's needed.
Remain untouched by life around you
Let not lesser lives distract you.

How much better would our lives be
If the rules we learned were thus——
Know and celebrate your inner self.
Dig deep and find the fire.
Do or be what gives you passion.
Let smiles and sadness light your face,
Encourage others to share themselves.
Make each day a joy to greet.
Open your heart to what others feel.
Let peace touch your soul.
Embrace and live the life around you.

THE AWAKENING

My mind can be a lonely place.
The same thoughts going round and round.
The mantra of self-absorption playing continuously
Drowning out the sounds of life.
I cannot hear above the din
Of the many thoughts rushing through my mind
Crowding out my desperate need for calm.

Suddenly I'm overwhelmed,
The spinning thoughts shatter my semblance of control.
I cannot sustain the mounting tension gripping my inner core.
Pent up energy courses through my body
Seeking a way to expend its force.
Some unknown will takes possession,
Emotions escape their bonds,
Tears begin to flow,
Cries of release escape my lips.

The flood gates open
I struggle to close the gap.
This is not a comfortable place for me.
Some deep need fights the closure.
The escaping cries are more haunting.
They rise as if my life is threatened.
I cannot shut this feeling down,
There is more to me than what I knew.
Calm settles as the cries become quiet sobs.
From this awakening a new spirit may emerge
With the love and care of those around me.

THE TEACHER

Could it be she changed my life
From what it might have been?
I was only nine years old when I was chosen
To be the target of her control.

What threat could I have been?
A young boy eager to pursue my love of learning
Expecting a teacher to share that yearning
With words of encouragement and gentle urgings.

She was not the kind of teacher I had known
She ranted and shouted and attacked with words
She made me feel small
She called me "mister know it all".

Attempting control she lost control
Behind her back respect collapsed
School was not a happy place to be
Her words confused and made me tremble.

She only had four months to wreak her havoc
Four months of fear
Four months of being told
Don't be who you are.

She never understood
The last day she cried
She looked at me and asked
"How would she survive?"

What she'd done was now my fault
Her life was now a part of me
If only I hadn't challenged her
She would have kept control

Years later these memories linger
They hurt and make me sad.

NOW I WAIT

The decision for surgery is made
The date is set, the waiting begins.
For over a year the pain has been there
From hip to ankle and between.
Sometimes fleeting, sometimes breath-taking.
Each step is carefully taken
Anticipating what may send the pain cascading,
Wresting my thoughts from what's around me

At its worst, it could consume me
Make me cry out for relief
I'd take the pills to kill the pain
Leaving me suspended in space.
Stretching and walking seemed to work
I can live with this I thought
Until the morning the fire returned
Burning again from waist to toe.

It was time to find a new solution
Face down my fear of intervention.
Enough time has passed
I want it gone
The date is set.
Now I wait!

BENEATH THE CALM

Reason and intellect have subdued my feelings
Clothed them with a seeming calm.
A raging torrent of pent up energy struggles to emerge.
I've lived my life with only glimpses
Of that which hides within
I fear to let these passions free.
I know not what I may become.

No longer can I wait
My emotion and intellect must intertwine,
To find the peace to cast my fear away
To let my spirit soar.

MASSAGE

His fingers probe deep within my neck
I feel the energy start to build
A gentle flow starts at my toes
Just below the surface it caresses up my body
Through my legs, my thighs, my groin
Over my belly, through my chest
My face warms, my breathing deepens
It envelops every part of me
My back arches
My neck presses deeper into his hands
The energy shudders through my body
My legs vibrate without control
One, two, three times it erupts
More, more, more my body shouts
And then it's gone
My body rests
My breathing slows
I feel spent and alive at once
My neck sinks into his hands
As relaxation warms my core

A MOMENT IN TIME

A quiet stillness settles
My body resonates with the beating of my heart
I sense every part of me connected each to the other
An aura of simmering energy languishes around me
I await the next sound to thrust through the barrier of silence
Will that sound tease from me a new thought?
Will it shatter this relaxed peacefulness?
Will it take me deeper into tranquillity?
Can I shut out all those sounds
And live completely in this space in time?
Unlikely!

As I continue to move through my life
These tranquil interludes are oft too far between
I will relish this moment while it lasts
I know not what the next sound may be.

THE UNWRITTEN SPEECH

What words will come tomorrow
When I stand there before them?
What path will my thoughts go down
As I search their eyes for what they want to hear?
Is it information they seek
Or re-assurance that all is well?
Do they want to be entertained?
Do they want a gentle reminder of the world around them?
Each of these I can do depending on the mood
That fills the room and spirits me on the path.
It would be easier to choose before I begin
But spontaneity is what adds the thrill
That engages the audience with me.
What's my niche now that I'm on my own?
My niche is being who I am.
Challenging, seeing what needs to be done.
Willing to share myself with them
In hopes of achieving common ground.
They'll remember the personal parts of me
And woven through will be the thoughts I leave.
I will establish the rapport and connect.
The words will come to fill the message
I chose to leave.

WORDS

Words, words, words fill our lives
They flow effortlessly from some
Hesitatingly from others
They can praise, explain, condemn
Impact your senses with unexpected force
Build your confidence
Delight yourself and those around you
Touch those who know you not.
Unspoken words can haunt your friendships
Shared words can deepen love
Sharp words can tear your past asunder
Words alone are nothing
Tone and context make them live
Listen carefully to how others hear and feel your words
Do they hear you as you are?

THE FLOW OF WORDS

Sitting here pencil in hand
I wait for that one phrase
To fleetingly cross my mind
To begin the flow of words
From the hidden confines of my mind.
The pencil moves across the page
Recording these thoughts
Sometimes without hesitation
Other times with long pauses between the words.
I know not from where these words come.
Like bubbles of air escaping from the bed of a stream
They gently rise to the surface
Releasing their energy in a burst of consciousness.
Words unspoken but destined to appear on paper
To express a thought
To paint a picture
To display a secret emotion
To touch the heart of another.
I need to let these words flow
To be surprised at how they look on paper
To feel the way they sound when read
To share them with others around me.
What a surprise it is
To find a secret part of oneself
Now able to feel the warm delight
Of new found pleasure in what I do

FREEDOM

A newborn child needs no words
To tell you how they feel.
Emotions rule their life and yours with them.
A cry, a smile tells it all
Love flows unspoken
There is no inherent need to hide their feelings.
They learn this tactic as they grow.
How can we be who we are
If that part of us is battened down?
We temper our joy
We hide our fears
We keep our sadness within ourselves.
How much better would our lives be
If we were to embrace and celebrate the emotional part of us
And, like a child, let it free?

MY OPEN HAND

In a moment of silence
I look carefully at my open hand.
I see for the first time
That which has been part of me my whole life.
The symmetry is amazing.
The lines stretch and merge across my palm.
I can feel energy moving out towards the tips of my fingers.
My pulse beats evenly.
Slowly the fingers of my other hand
Lightly touch the lines and contours.
They trace the shape and outline of each finger
They gently caress the texture of my palm
A warm glowing sensation envelops my hand.

RECALL THE SOUNDS

It seems but a short time ago
Children's laughter filled our home.
Now they've gone
Moved on to lives of their own
The space seems empty without their sounds
What were those sounds that have fled?
    ...demanding cries of a hungry baby
    ...bubbling babbles of an energetic toddler
    ...triumphant rings of first sentences
    ... never-ending questions of a precocious four year old
    ... proudly heralded accomplishments of first days at school
    ... joy of friendships bouncing from the walls
    ... quiet whispers between sisters
    ... hushed tones of a mother expressing her love
    ... challenging forthrightness of an emerging teen
    ... soothing words of shared experience
    ... unspoken words of teenage angst
    ... confident tones of emerging adults
    ... flashes of fear for what lies ahead
We have heard it all
This music in the background of our lives

At times we listened carefully
At other times we made too much noise.
Now they're gone
The melody has faded into the memories of our minds
Ready to be summoned forth once again
When the mood is right to let these memories play
To once again recall those sounds
That filled our home and lives

IMAGES

What images will I see today
Through the windows of my mind
Some will be those conjured up from my past
Some will be what I view the future to be
Some will be the ones I see around me
Too few will be the ones I feel deep inside

It takes anxious energy to view the past
To re-live the mistakes I've made
To find the missed solutions
The past cannot be changed
I'll keep only those memories that build my spirit up
I'll let the others drift away

The images of future waste my time
I cannot control what tomorrow brings
Some unforeseen circumstance will intrude
To change what might have been
Too much focus on my future
Limits what I can see today

I want to live within the present
Expending energy to see and feel the moment
Living this day to its fullest
Brings me closer to a gentle wholeness
The choice is mine to make
I will choose the images to see

IN SEARCH OF FRIENDS

Within this sprawling piece of suburbia,
Newly built but not yet home,
Strangers had gathered in search of friends.
Children playing apprehensively in the den.
Adults conversing in tentative tones
Looking for connection to build a friendship.
Where are you from? What do you do?
All those questions asked and answered.
Suddenly the room was quiet.
All conversation eerily ceased.
That awkward moment of emptiness in chatter had come.
No one knew what to say.
Had all the hopes for connection fled?
A child's laughter breaks the silence.
It gives new focus of things to say.
Slowly, hopefully the conversations re-engage.
They've found a common thread to build new friendships.

DREAMS

It is breathtaking to awake from a dream so real.
My heart is pounding
My hands and body are wet with unearned sweat
For a brief flash of time, I feel lost
The dream images are still clear and sharp but too quickly fade
Consciousness reasserts itself
Taking me to the real world
But is this the real world in which I live
Or simply what I perceive it to be?
A merging of touch, smell, sight, taste and sound
To create images of reality in my mind.
Are these images any more real than those of my dreams?
What is the line between these worlds?

Need there be a line?
If there is no line then reality cannot be defined.
Every person sees their own real world
As a reflection of their experience and the images they create.
Perhaps, if my dreams stayed with me longer
I would better understand the sense of my reality
And let it be more easily influenced by what I feel.
Perhaps, my dreams are there
Simply to challenge my view
To give my mind the chance
To wander unleashed from my control
So when my senses encounter something new
They are free to create new perspectives of reality
Unimpeded from where I've been within myself.
Perhaps, there is no need of explanation
Dreams may only be a part of how a body functions
A chance to release energy unrestricted while sleep deepens
A time to let the mind rest and free fall through space.
There is no need for explanation.
Each of us has our dreams and they belong to us alone
But oh how exciting it would be
To see and feel another's dreams.
Somehow, I imagine it would be
Like opening a new level of consciousness
Of who and what we are within our real world.

WHO WE ARE

All too often we shelter who we are
Within the shadows of our lives.
We encapsulate our inner fears
Within an impermeable shell of nonchalance.
We hide our vulnerability
Behind a mask of false confidence.
We perpetuate the myth of calmness
Despite the angst that grips us.
We are two within one ——
One is what others see
The other is the one we feel.

This is not how our lives should be!
A single self feels no torment!
There is no need to battle our inner spirit
When it's part of what others see and hear.
Experience has taught us to hide our feelings
Uncertainty, sadness, anger, fragility if exposed
Threaten how others see us.
Easier for us to ignore our feelings
And not overstep the cultural limits of interaction.
We must not let this be our inherent response
To limit the person we can become.
We must join those who share themselves
Let them see who we are.
No more shadows, no more fears
We must be one with ourselves.

SURGERY APPROACHES

As the day for surgery approaches
Those useless "what ifs" start running through my mind.
They invade my dreams and intrude upon my waking thoughts
Threatening to kidnap me from the present
Into the abyss of self inflicted fear.
This is not a productive way to pass the time.
I've tried the less invasive cures
To rid myself of pain.
I know I cannot live this way.
Why can I not face the day
With only confidence in the outcome?
I must confront these fears and stare them down.
Calm the racing of my mind
Reassure myself all is right
Trust my instinct and not give in to fear.
I know the risks and think they're small
I know the pain will pass.
Acknowledging this fear will help to lessen
The swirling haunting of my thoughts

SIDE BY SIDE

I see them walking along the path
Mother and daughter side by side
Slightly stooped, Jessica moves with shortened pace
Matching the tentative steps beside her

Too small to clasp a hand
Leila holds a single finger
Not yet courageous enough
To walk alone without connection

All too soon their strides will lengthen
The tightly held hand will strain
To be released so she can explore
Along the path her mother chose

The day will come when independence will assert itself
Leila will take a path alone
Knowing her mother showed her the way
To adventure on her own

Even when that day arrives
The bond between them will not be broken
Leila will run home
To share her exploration and new found delights
With the person who first walked with her
Down her path of life

BAILEY

She lies in the middle of the room
Lost in a reverie of her silent dreams
Legs outstretched so each is grounded to the floor
A gentle stretch expands her toes
Her upright ears flick as if searching for an elusive sound
To draw her senses alert to impending danger
A vestige of the wild her ancestors lived in
Her chin lies tucked between her paws
At moments like this she ignores me
I am there to meet her needs
She'll come to me when hunger calls
Or when she wants a gentle, reassuring pat
Seldom will she seek me out
She is a dependent, independent beast
Whose eyes grow large when she's in a tear
Chasing some imaginary prey
Up the stairs, around the chair, across the room
The wild part of her conflicts with what she is
A cat who deigns to live with us

MY PLACE

What is my place?
 I pass through the consequence of time
searching for the meaning
The sounds of life play hauntingly in the background
My mind contemplates the reasons
for being in this void
Do I seek
a new purpose and direction
for the next phase of my existence
within a tumult of opportunity and choice?...

Transition brought me to this place
of insightful reconsideration of where I've been
I've been a person dwelling
within a shell that others see
Behind the mask of confidence and reason
hides an emotional self
waiting to share the words and poetry of life.

THE COUNSELLOR

I feel confident in my role in others' lives.
To listen and help them understand where they are
Within the lives they've lived till now.
They come to see me in times of crisis
Searching for understanding of how they feel
Caught up in who they've been.
They know not how to express the space they're in
They need to talk and be gently nudged
Along the path that's right for them.
I search and probe
Looking for a way to help them move.
I take risks in what I say
But if it's wrong
We'll choose another path along the way.
Our conversations change direction
As we unlock the spirit that is within them.
It's a pleasure to see the light go on
It's sad when they won't let me in.
Only they can make that choice
I can only try my best
To help them find their way.

MUSIC

Music reflects the melody of our lives
It resonates with all the emotions we feel
It can be...
> the joyous sound of rapture
> the melancholy whisper of sadness felt
> the staccato anger of emotions burst
> the warming heartbeat of developing love
> the gentle passion of emerging freedom
> the pounding fear of the unknown
> the terrible searing of misdirected jealousy
> the shared laughter of friendship
> the quiet pride in your children's lives

All part and parcel of who we are
Music plays constantly in the background of our lives
In a moment of quiet contemplation
Its melody can make us feel
We dwell within the sound itself

THE MELODY

Where goes my spirit
When I listen to the melody of music
Played against the sounds of nature?
The gentle strings amongst the songs of birds.
I feel the sound within my breast
It overwhelms my conscious and unconscious mind
I feel as if I can soar.
The gentle strains flood me with a wave of calm
I can feel every part of me ...
> ...the gentle beating of my heart
> ...the blood pulsing through my veins
> ...each breath filling my lungs
> ...the sensation of life in my fingertips

Music unleashes within me
Each part that makes me whole.

THE HUNGRY ONES

What thoughts hide behind those hungry eyes,
Children abandoned by the world,
Left to exist at the whim of others.
What brought them to this place?
Parents consumed by turmoil of war,
Families ravished by death from illness,
Homes destroyed by nature's fury,
Communities lost to globalization.
No matter the cause it's all come down
To fear and sadness merged to hopelessness in their eyes.
No hope of future, no love of family
No tomorrow, only the hunger and cold of today.
Where have we gone wrong?
We can fund huge armies
We can explore the stars
We can build great wealth
But we cannot nurture the children of the world
What blindness allows us to let this happen?
Cannot we see the inhumanity?
Cannot we look beyond our wants to meet their needs?
The world has become a selfish place ignoring a simple truth.
Those hungry abandoned children who survive
Become angry desperate adults of tomorrow
Prepared to tear the world asunder
To take what others have.
If that is not a legacy we want
Solutions must be found.
It will need a new awakening
To fill those children's eyes with hope
For food, peace and love.

THE FALLS

The mist rises like steam from a giant cauldron
Blocking out the view of nature's power.
You feel the tremor of bursting energy beneath your feet
The sound vibrates through your body
Your eyes strain to see the source.
Slowly the wind changes direction
The mist is blown away
Revealing the majesty of falling water
Disappearing into the abyss below.
It has been drawn inexplicably along its path
Through field and forest and stream
To the river that sealed its journey to this place.
Where it will free fall through space
To join the flow again.

How like our lives this water flow
Constrained along the path we chose
Without warning sudden unexpected tumult appears
Our lives are suspended momentarily on the brink of time
Freedom is ours
As we tumble through this space
We are free to choose new direction
Before we join the flow again.

ISOLATION

We live our lives isolated in this time and place
surrounded by those who care for us
immune to the needs around us...
>   the need for human touching
>   the need for kind words
>   the need for understanding
>   the need for acceptance

We shut our eyes, too afraid to see.
Is it fear of connection
or simply a life made too busy
by tasks that have no meaning?
Look at how young children play
before they learn our rules.
They touch, they listen, they care
oblivious to colour of skin, language spoken, or economic place
We need to live our childhood ways ...
>   break down the barriers
>   make connections and feel the needs
>   embrace the world around us
>   live a life beyond ourselves

SPRING AWAITS

I look upon my world with delight.
On the brink of spring a new day has dawned.
Anticipation waits to burst forth in a blanket of green.
Winter is holding us tenaciously in its grip
Surprising us with late storms.
Soon the crocuses will open their wings of colour
To herald the stirring within the earth.
Among the swelling buds perch returned songbirds.
Hawks circle lazily in the warm breezes.
The fields lie patiently waiting the planting of new seeds.
They want to once again feel the warm tentacles of roots
Seeking nurture and foundation within their depths.
They yearn to be awash with warm spring rains.

The hibernation is almost over
Be patient!
The cycle of nature will once again
Present to us a new spring
The sun will warm our faces
Songs will fill the air
The young will emerge
Our spirits will soar
Our hearts will warm
Each new dawn will be a new beginning

Feel the warm breezes
Smell the fragrance of new life
Be one with mother earth

TODAY SHE'S TWENTY

Today she's twenty
How can this be?
It seems only yesterday she was born
All arms and legs she emerged
To fill our world with her presence

Who is the woman she's become?
Others know her for who she is
We know her as the child we've seen grow
      ...a newborn cuddled in her mother's arms
      ...a tentative toddler's steps
      ...the hands between sisters held
      ...her first awaited words
      ...inconsolable crying in the car
      ...warm shy smiles
      ...her love of animals in her life
      ...Puffy her stuffed friend
      ...her thoughtful remembrance of those around her
      ...her demand to be herself
We know her for all her parts

Perhaps, someday these memories will fade
We will know her as others do
A woman of her own making
Who will be what she wants to be
Not what others expect
A child we raised to find her way
To be a woman content with who she is

FREEDOM TO WANDER

I'll let my mind wander to see where it may go
Will it anticipate the future or will it dwell upon the past?
What grand scheme can it envisage?
What minute detail can it contemplate?
Can it focus or only leap from thought to thought?
Too often I limit the search within safe constraints
Unsure of being challenged by thoughts beyond my control.

Minds free to search without limitation
Find a treasure trove of new dimensions to pursue.
Unexpected opportunities for growth present themselves
Solutions to unsolved mysteries magically appear
Unexpected associations between reality and emotion emerge
New challenges blossom to enrich our lives

But not today!
My mind chooses only to live in this moment
Untouched by grander more intimate pursuits
It enjoys the peaceful melody playing in the background
Not searching either forward or back
Content to be at rest.

CONNECTION

Look around in a crowd of unrecognizable faces.
What thoughts and feelings are hidden behind those masks?
What tears are being shed in the confines of their hearts?
What smiles are being shielded?
Every one of those faces is
the outward visage of a secret self
wishing to share what lies behind their eyes.
Searching for a friendly face to welcome a kindred soul.
Can a connection be made
between two solitary individuals in this crowded room?
A questioning look, a cautious smile may appear.
A silent whisper of need may escape
seeking an ear attuned to secret sound
within the crowded space.

THE OTHER SIDE OF SURGERY

I hear a whisper calling me back
from the hallucinations that have hijacked my dreams.
It's hard to leave this dimension in which I find myself.
The anaesthetics and pain controllers
 have opened this strange world.
It's like a dream yet unlike a dream.
My mind is seemingly on many conscious tracks simultaneously
The lines of reality are blurred
I jump from one track to the other without hesitation
People appear, then suddenly vanish
Replaced by the next group to pass through my room
Aware of me, inquisitive as to who I am,
but they do not know me.
Human shapes evolve into inanimate objects.
Bubbles appear quivering as if alive,
graciously floating along the bed rail,
up the intravenous pole and gently bounce to the ceiling
until they disappear into the distance.
In the background play the sounds of the hospital routine,
there but not there.
A whispering nurse informs me of a new invasion to my body
but who am I to care, I'm not here at this moment.
I'm standing at a distance,
Watching, trying to connect myself to one of these realities.
I am only an actor
playing this role as patient in an elaborate play of life.
That explains the unreal nature of what I see
It's only a play; my real life begins as soon as this act is over.
I clamber up through the depths of consciousness
struggling to return to the real place.
I am now awake with part of me in each world,
the real world and the other.
I have never visited this other world.

This dimension goes beyond the "what if" unreal world
that my mind can conjure from day to day.
It does not distort reality,
it takes absolute possession.
As I battle, it tries to draw me back.
My mind fights to assert a semblance of control
I return to the surface, back in my world,
plagued with jumbled flashbacks to where I've been.
It has taken days for my thoughts to settle
where I can now describe
where I've been.
Through the other side of surgery
where a deep dark collision of reality and hallucination
overpowered my sense of being.
This line between sanity and insanity
an unnerving place to be
a place where panic overwhelms
more painful than the body's pain.

GRADUATION

Your spirit soars high
As you begin a new phase of your life
Full of optimism
Longing for it to be all that is expected
New friends to be made
New situations to experience
New opportunities to embrace
New fears to overcome
Will there be surprises in this new life?
Undoubtedly!
Behind every door that opens
Lies an unexplored part of what you will become.
The past will be your anchor
A secure base from which to begin the exploration
Providing stability when unease intrudes upon your life.
However, the past must not your future be
Enjoy each day
Make choices that enrich your life and the lives around you
The present is for living
The future is never sure
The past is what you were, not what you are
Relish in the opportunity that is yours
Take time to be at peace with the person you've become
When the time is right seize the next step along your path
If it's not right
Try again
The world waits for you to take your place.

PEACEFUL STILLNESS

I feel a peaceful stillness
Has captured my spirit and set it free
From the constraints which were self imposed.
A result of how I viewed myself.
Too much reason, not enough feeling
Too much expectation, not enough satisfaction
Too much hurry, not enough contentment.
My world had become too much outside myself.

It's not important what we do
We are valued for who we are
Our place will be in the memories of family and friends.
Are we there when needed?
Do we help them to be themselves?
Do we smile or frown?
Are we a person they'd like to be?
Are we content with who we are?

I'm glad I've learned this lesson of living
It is now up to me to battle the whispers of the past
That will surely try
To contain my spirit and prevent it from roaming free.

I NEED NO MASK

Behind the disguise of tranquillity, a tumult of thoughts boil
Giving no rest to the person behind the mask.
My greatest fear is to be seen for who I am
Uncertain and insecure.
It seems surreal that so much emotion can be contained
Within the confines of my mind.
Trapped, surging to escape but totally constrained
By the sturdy façade of unreal self-imposed normalcy.
The more emotions held within
The greater the turmoil builds
Thoughts collide, an endless cycle of re-generation
The pent-up energy builds
The pace and tension cannot find release
The body begins to shatter
Decisions cannot be made
Sleep becomes a phantom that cannot be found
Adrenaline rushes become a surge of anxiety
The body revolts.
This is not a sustainable place in which to live
A frantic search begins
To find a new truth
A place of balance, a place to feel again.
It cannot be found alone
Someone must be there
To listen and hear the cry for a new sense of self
To open the doors to a new understanding of
Who am I?
What have I become?
Who do I wish to be?
With her help, I meld the parts of me into a person
Content with whom I am
Secure in my feeling of self
Calm in face of turmoil
Balanced and aware of the emotions that are part of me
A person who needs no masks
To hide what lies within
For I have become one with my entire being
I feel at peace.

OUR WORLD

The spring sun shimmers through the glass
Warming the back of my hand as I sit
Searching for words to write upon this paper.
Words that when connected will reflect
The world in which we live-

A wonderful and desperate place
shaped by each of us who live upon its surface.
Where conflict often rules the day.
Where love and harmony seem beyond our human reach.

We struggle for such love and harmony within our lives,
our families, our communities, our countries.
It becomes more fragile as the circle widens.
For some it cannot be found even within themselves.
Lines that separate us from these needs are sharply drawn
between race, religion, and language.
Based on what we've learned,
greed not need sets many priorities.
A society unwilling to find solutions beyond historic rules.

There is no grand resolution to the inadequacies of our world.
Only small steps each of us can take
to expand our lives
to recognize the needs of those who elsewhere live
to think beyond our small space.
Hope exists to embrace this challenge
to make the world a better place
for each of those who follow us
into what has been our world.

MY POEMS

These poems seem to have come
From a part of me I did not know.
It's as if another person inside yet outside of me
Has released this torrent of words
To describe where I've been and where I am.
They paint a picture of what I see and feel around me
With an amazing imagery and vibrancy I did not know I saw.
It's amazing to meet a part of yourself
That neither you nor others have known.
I'm happy to have found the combination
To unlock this in me.
How many others are waiting for their spirit to be freed
To feel and express the emotions locked within?
Will I be able to keep this freedom
As I venture forth once again into my world
Where our culture frowns on being free?
A culture based on fear
Fear of touch, fear of connection
Why have we locked up what makes us human?
Perhaps by sharing what I've learned
Others will be willing to take the risk
To let their emotions see the day.
What a gentler place our small corner of the world will be
If such can be my gift.

NEW FRONTIERS

It's a challenge to search out new frontiers in our lives
New intellectual pursuits that exist beyond our norm
New emotional edges to experience
New beginnings to lift our spirits higher.
For most it's easier to stay well within the limitations they know.
These boundaries to their lives seem so high
To even peer timidly over them is too great a risk.
A risk to how they see themselves
A risk of not knowing what lies ahead.
Better to accept the person they think they know
Than release a hidden yearning
Which disturbs their rigid, complacent place.

THE RITE OF SPRING

The spring winds wash through the treetops
No sound of rustling leaves
The buds are just emerging.
The trees sway gently to and fro
Stretching to feel the warmth blowing past.
The forest floor wears its first shroud of green.
The low shrubs are tinged with colour.
Birds perched in the yet forlorn branches call tentatively.
Frogs are boisterous in their longing to greet new mates.
Footprints of deer mark the damp earth.
Racoons stealthily search for food.
First insects wing through the shimmering rays of sun.
The longer I stand without moving
The more sounds magically are heard
As the creatures of nature
Welcome the season of renewal.

MUSIC OF MY SOUL

I can feel the music in the tips of my fingers
As if I could sit down and play the melody
But alas, I do not know how to play
The lessons were wasted in my youth
When other things seemed more important
Than mechanically learning how to find the notes
I never felt the music like I feel it now
It's connected deep within my being
It plays upon the chords of my emotions
Calling them forth so I can feel the tender edges
Of what can only be the music of my soul

TIME TO PAUSE

Calm and quietness surround me.
High above a solitary contrail marks the passing
Of a jet filled with people in a hurry to arrive.
Do they know their destination
Or like most of life will it be just a brief stop
Before moving on, never sure where our spirit lives?
Is home the place that family dwells
Or simply another transient stop to rest awhile
Before venturing forth to see what the new day brings?
We are always in a hurry to the next place in our lives
As if it is not fulfilling to simply rest and enjoy the present.
We spend so much time planning
Our next moves on the chessboard of life
We forget where we've been
And what have been our greatest pleasures
   –the love of family and friends grounded in the moment
   –the warm satisfaction of providing comfort and companionship
   –the peace of allowing our minds to be in a place of nothingness
   –not striving for excellence and challenge every waking moment
We need to pause to refresh ourselves for the frantic pace.
For some the pause will provide an impetus
To find a better balance
That nurtures both them and those whose lives they touch.

BEYOND MY CONTROL

What is the driving force that takes me down this path?
To take responsibility for things beyond my influence
Am I seeking approval from those around me?
Does my ego need stroking?
Why can I not be satisfied with what I can achieve?
Why drive myself beyond the possible to the impossible?
I cannot lead others' lives

I cannot influence what lies beyond my sphere
But that does not dissuade me from trying
And feeling responsible if I fail.
Perhaps I've never really drawn the line
Between my responsibility and those of the larger group
Or am I a person who simply sees things in a broader context
Then fails to separate the vision from my responsibility for action.
Is that why I never seem satisfied with what can be done today?
Who will do it if not me?
Some may say this pattern is built on low self-esteem
Rather I wonder if it is an expectation
Of self esteem beyond human dimension –
An expectation beyond reasonable possibility.
For those of us caught up in this way of acting
A lesson must be learned
We must be satisfied with what we can achieve
Not be embroiled in the unachievable.
This is a confusing cycle we find ourselves in
We can see beyond ourselves
But must draw the line on what we can do
To feel satisfied and complete at the end of the day.
We must share our visions
And let others take them into action.
We must accept that we are only human
A small cog in the vast wheel of life
That will continue turning whether or not we are there.
We must rest assured we've done our bit
The world is not our stage.

HARMONY

For most of my life, my intellect has ruled
It has strategized, evaluated, and chosen my way
It never felt secure
There was little peace at each day's end
One's emotional self becomes isolated as intellect rules the day
The joy of laughter fades
The pain of sadness is gradually hidden away
Connection is made but without the human touch
Intellect is not enough to sustain us in our lives
Our spirit needs both parts of us in harmony
To make us one within ourselves
To let us face each day with a smile upon our face
To touch another and feel content
To find our place and be at peace
This is how our lives should be
Our intellect will still be free to roam
Searching out all our possibilities
With the security of knowing
We will feel all the emotional intricacies
Of the life we choose to lead

THE LANE

I've walked this lane many times in my life.
As a child it was the path to new adventure
It led me to exploration of nature's splendour.
I followed it to the creek
To stand in the cool flowing water inches from my boot tops.
I walked barefoot basking in the summer sun
The pebbles on its surface making me dance in place.
I wobbled side to side as I learned to cycle its length.
I've walked hand in hand with the one I love
I've held my children's hands as they began their explorations
Like the generations before them.
I've walked many times contemplating the twists and turns of life.
It's a path of familiarity
With clear direction but unknown mental destination.
Each of us needs such a place to walk
To think and be aware.

THE APRIL DAY

I listen carefully to the sounds around me.
On this calm sunny April day.
I am in the bush clearing
Isolated from the sounds of everyday life
Except for the gentle rumble of the jet flying high overhead.
The insects frantically buzz near me
Trying to decide what brought me to their place.
The black winged flies dive by my face as if on attack
But turn away at the last moment.
The hawk soars majestically it's wings spread wide
To catch the updraft of a gentle spring breeze.
Birds call through the branches to one another
In tentative but persistent tones.
The dried grass of yesteryear stands mute
Against the emerging green of new growth.
The wind-strewn seeds of last fall have settled
Into the warm clutch of the earth.
The water in the creek gently meanders on its way
Gurgling over small rocks and swirling in small eddies.

The air is alive with anticipation
I feel I am part of this great re-emergence
Refreshing the earth
Bringing forth promise of new hope
Allowing re-creation of life
An opportunity to create ourselves anew
As we open our hearts and minds
To the miracle of spring

ANXIETY ATTACK

Suddenly it's there
The overwhelming feeling of nausea and light- headedness.
It can come unexpectedly at any time
Driving the car, sitting at the kitchen table
In the middle of the night, during a conversation
Surely it can be seen on my face
My heart quickens, I cannot breathe
Is it a heart attack?
Am I dying?
Am I breaking down?
All these thoughts flash through my mind
Then it passes
I feel drained
My mind is jumbled
My personal demon squeezes me tighter and tighter
More and more frequently it seizes me
I anticipate its appearance with both acceptance and dread
What a way to live!
Anxiety attacks have taken possession of my every day

My body is crying out for respite
From stress, from worry, from too much nervous energy
From all the things that can haunt me day to day
Unresolved tensions, pent-up emotions, striving beyond my abilities
My human frailties suppressed beyond reason.
I must embrace each part of who I am
Face the panic
Recognize it for what it is
A warning that all is not well
Search out the cause
Relax
Deal with the hidden stresses
Breathe deeply
Share my fears
Do not let them be bigger than they are.
The anxiety will lessen and eventually disappear
But I must be aware
It lies in hiding waiting to re-attack.

FAMILY

A family is a safe harbour.
A refuge from cares that confound us
A place for reminiscing and laughter
We gather together to share
Our lives, our hopes, our failures
Rejoicing in having each other
To accept each as they are
Within the circle of love.

SEARCHING

Searching, searching, searching
For that elusive key
To unlock the mysteries of my life
To open the door to a clear understanding
Of where I fit.
Behind that door a vast plethora of answers must exist
Waiting to be embraced
If not, then why have I been searching?

Too often we seek what cannot be found
There is no key, no hidden door
We can only live each day within the present
There are no magical answers.

LIVING OUR INNER SELF

Do others see us for who we are?
Are our inner selves different?
Some argue we are not what others see
Rather what we feel and know to be inside is our true self.
If we know who we are
Then others will know the same.
It will not be hidden away behind a façade
Created for the world to see.
Not all will see us clearly
Their perspective will be clouded
By their own lives and limitations.
We will be comfortable to be known by how others see us
When we live our inner self.

SETBACK

Today is filled with
Too much worry, too much focus
On the pain that has re-appeared.
It's not the same but close enough
To fear the surgery has been a failure.
Perhaps it's just a minor setback
Inflammation caused by who knows what.
It's enough to challenge my ability
To focus out beyond myself.
If nothing else these last four weeks
I've found it can be solved.
I'll back off the physio and consult again
To see if we can find the fix.
A few days rest may be enough
For it to pass away.
I hope that's so
Another bout would be a major struggle.
It will take perseverance and willingness
To accept what lies ahead.

MOVING ON

Suddenly I'm ready
To move on
To leave this void and resume the transition
To the next phase of my life.
It's taken time
To face the demons I've created in my mind
  My sense of over responsibility
  My need for control
  My inability to celebrate my achievements
  An ego that sometimes needed stroking
  An intellect that overrode my emotions.
Characteristics that entrapped me
With their insidious seductiveness
To create an outer shell around myself.
I'm now more comfortable with who I am
More willing to share myself
Striving to emerge from the fog of fear
That hid myself from others.
This has not been an easy journey
It brought me to the brink of meltdown
But I am fortunate to have
A spouse who eased me through the dark spot
A family prepared to give their love
Friends who encouraged me
A counsellor who challenged me to find my way.
Though my life will now move on.
I must be mindful
Not to settle back into the old routines
Allowing a private self to once again take refuge
Within the shadows of my mind

TIME

In the background of our lives
Runs the relentless clock of time
The one absolute over which we have no control
We grow older with each heartbeat of time
The present becomes the past in a flash
There is always a future and a past
Only one present moment of time
How we use our time as mortal beings is ours to determine
We can fret about what the future brings
We can anguish about the past
We can be dissatisfied about the present
Or we can look to the future with joy
Remember the past with pleasure
Celebrate the present
It's ours to choose
Time will have passed us by if we hesitate
To lead a life that when our time is passed
There is no regret, no sorrow for what we might have done

A SPLASH OF YELLOW

Suddenly they're there
As if overnight, some unseen hand
Has waved a wand to create their presence.
We dig them, we spray them
They resist human control
They hid in the fencerows
Maturing to caste their immortality to the winds.
They have lain patiently
Beneath the cold surface of winter
Waiting to burst forth
To blanket the fields and lawns with yellow
To taunt us with their splash of colour
To dare us once again to take up the unending battle
Against this valiant soldier of nature.

THE HUMMINGBIRDS

The hummingbirds have arrived
to drink hastily from the feeder
as they flit from perches unseen
among the unfolding leaves of the maple tree.
They flash by in their flight
a shimmering iridescent green
to suddenly stop and hover in one spot.
They're wary of the hungry cats
basking in the warm sun close but distant to the feeder.
With courage mustered they wing in to feed
drink hungrily then dash away
to return suddenly from a new direction.
There are at least three
which means repeated attacks
as each attempts to feed.
Not willing to share
they each, in turn, master momentary control.
How can something so small move so aggressively and quickly?
Their beating wings a blur to the human eye.
A miracle of nature
returned once again to amuse and surprise us with their antics

BEYOND THE STARS

We are so small compared to what lies beyond the stars
No doubt something else exists within our galaxy
Some intelligence inhabits those other places
There is no reason to believe we are alone
We are naïve to think ourselves the superior beings
In the infinity of time other life forms will have evolved
Where, we know not
The day will come
When we shall meet
Perhaps not in a physical form familiar to our being
Rather some metaphysical experience
To challenge our concept of life.
Will we be ready
To take ourselves beyond our human limits
To appreciate and accept a new form of life
That must exist out beyond the stars?

PLANTING TIME

It's May
Time for planting this year's harvest
The seed remains in the bags
Too wet, too cool.
The farmers pace the fields
Checking to see if they're dry and warm.
No such luck!
They peer at the sky
Willing the clouds and rain to disappear
Quietly pleading for the sun to break through.
The tension of pent-up energy of man and machine
Almost palpable throughout the countryside.
Waiting, waiting.
Tension rises, tempers flare at little things.
Dependent on nature's whims

Unable to do anything but wait
Each passing day lessens their resilience.
Little chance now of that perfect year
Of moisture, sun, and heat
To bring forth a bountiful harvest
To be remembered in those years like this
When once again they wait and fret
The rains will continue unabated
The seed unplanted.
It's never happened, but when they're in this limbo
All is possible in their mind.
But wait!
The sun is out
It feels warmer
The wind is drying out the land
Start the tractors
Fill the seed hoppers
They've made it through this impasse of nature
They're rolling again
There's still time for it to be a good year

THE SUN'S WARMTH

The sun finally appears through the scattered cloud
To warm the day and raise the spirits
Of those depressed by the weather doldrums.
Their spirit has been as grey as the world around them.
Each day lacked the sparkle to ignite them.
Today the rays provide the needed impetus
To spark their optimism
For each new day ahead.

THE WAVE OF EMOTION

From what part of my well of emotions flows this feeling
That floods me when I least expect it.
My eyes fill with tears
A deep sadness seems to strangle my spirit.
It lasts but a few seconds and then passes
Like a small wave washed ashore unexpectantly from a calm lake.

It has been trapped and building within me forever
Only now am I allowing it
To rise like bubbles of trapped air
Floating energetically to the surface.
The pent-up energy escapes
Free at last to join the fullness of freedom.

What is this emotion?
Is it grief for the past, for things that are gone
Or is it a glimpse
Into the complexity of my emotional self
Like a fleeting smile or a sudden deep laugh
Triggered by unexpected circumstance.

Sadness and grief are hidden
Seldom shared within the confines of our culture.
As I learn more about my true self
All my feelings are more fragile
Anxiously waiting to feel the light of day
Tired of being hidden in dark crevices.

I allow myself to feel the full range of my emotions
No matter how mysteriously they may suddenly seize me.
I accept them as being part of me
A sense of fullness fills my heart.
I feel as if I am discovering
What it means to be one with one's self.

RANDOM PASSAGES ON GRIEF

The grief has long been held
Buried deep within the contours of my soul
Waiting, waiting for a time to emerge
To touch my heart and make me whole

———o———

Grief must be explored to its true depth
Otherwise it lies hidden deep within the spirit
Creating an emotional imbalance
That impedes the smooth sailing of our lives

———o———

I must let this grief run its course
Put to rest the events and longings that were its source
Recognize that grief unexplored
Grips my soul in a tenacious hold
Confounding my ability to be at peace

———o———

Grief comes from many sources
From birth to death
We struggle to understand the losses we feel
Loss of opportunities
Loss of loved ones
Loss of childhood innocence
Loss of youth
Loss of parting and moving on
Loss of who we are
The list goes on and on
Some specific, some vague and indeterminate
Yet all profoundly impacting on our lives
We often hid these losses behind a superficial mask of tranquillity
Rather than exploring the grief, we shut it down

Or seek a blanket of comfort from those around us
To hide it from our view
We must grieve these changes in our lives
Otherwise subconsciously we continue to dwell in our past
Grief allows us to move into the present
It cleanses us of the events of the past
Once fully felt, fond memories emerge
To form the background to our present lives

———————o———————

Grief is part of who we are
As real as joy, love, and laughter
Feel the sadness and let it go
It cannot rule your life
Once you've let it free

———————o———————

Grief touches your inner spirit
It plays upon the heartstrings of your life
It is a reflection of what has been a part of your life
It allows you to acknowledge that past
It allows you to leave it all behind
To move forward with fond memories
No regrets, no unspoken words of love
Will haunt your daily life
If you've fully grieved and let it go

———————o———————

Grief becomes anger when held inside
The "might have beens" crowd our daily thoughts
We dwell upon our neglected opportunities
To express our love or seek new challenge
We failed to grieve our losses
And thus have not left those things behind us
We've grown old

We allowed our grief to fester deep inside
Until it has become an anger with life
How could this have happened to us?
Who can we blame?
We will die and not have been content with what has been our life
If this is not the life you want to live
Then feel your grief, express it, share it
Grow through it to the present
Live each day with no regrets

———o———

So many in our culture feel the grip of depression
They swallow the magic cures
They look no further to find a probable cause

For many, the unrequited grief stored deep within their soul
Has reached a saturation point
Where the human spirit can no longer thrive
The grief drowns out all other emotions that sustain them
It has been growing slowly throughout their lives
Like an unsuspected malignant tumour
Burrowing deep within their spirit
They've become exhausted with this burden they carry
The body says enough
The lights dim, depression deepens
The magic swallowed cures brighten the lights
But leave the burden of grief unopened
To truly return to life
They must open themselves to the grief stored within
Understand what it is they grieve
Explore its fullness
Feel its sadness
Go beyond it to the present
The darkness will lift
They will return to live their lives

THE FOUR AGREEMENTS

We watch but we don't see
We listen but we don't hear
We think but we don't feel
We're living lives that others created
Lives that are only dreams
Made up of the expectations of those
Who we know and knew
Parents, siblings, teachers, friends
We watch, we listen
We think we know who we are
Few of us see, hear and feel
The uniqueness of ourselves
We should seek that knowledge
And live a life within the present
Being impeccable with our word
Not making assumptions
Not taking what others say personally
Doing our best
The four agreements the Toltec spoke
A foundation on which to build our lives
Free from the dreams others made

GRADUATION DAY

Today our daughter graduated from university
Time has flown so fast
It seems only yesterday that I took that same walk.
Thirty-two years have passed
Years filled with challenges and opportunities
With joy and sadness
With the twists and turns of life.
With the love of family
Her life will also be filled with passing time
The same as the generations before us.
How she uses that time will fill her memories
It will create her image in others' minds
It will be the legacy of her life.
The consequence of time moves on
For her generation and those to follow.
Each will leave their mark if they live a life of usefulness
To self, to family, and to community.
We can ask no more of them
Than they walk through this open door
With spirit in their steps
With hope and optimism in their thoughts
With love in their hearts
With a smile on their face
Ready to create new experiences and happiness
In the life they live.

EMOTION

You feel the emotion waiting to erupt.
All your feelings meshed together
In an overwhelming depth of spirit
Like molten lava deep within the earth's core
Seeking a path to the light of day.

The time for containment is past
Which will it be?

A gradual awakening of the senses
An unexpected tear
A fleeting smile
A wanton splash of regret
An enveloping glow in your inner core
A warm embrace of each part of you
"Or"
A thunderous explosion of your senses
A molten outpouring of grief, anger, sadness, joy
A tangled web of raw emotion
Engulfing every part of you in its path
As it rushes through your being
Taking you to the edge of your space.

How much more comforting for the spirit
To be warmed by the gradual awakening of these emotions
Than by an angry eruption that can drown the sense of self.
Feel the flow begin
Feel its source in the centre of your being
Feel it radiate through your heart and mind
Feel its warmth flush your face
Feel it bring a rim of tears to your eyes
Feel all your emotions freely flow

Your spirit is awash with wholeness
Your heart and mind have become one
The warmth radiates from your being
You are content to be yourself

DECISIONS

Decisions are part of living
They are not always easy
Some are quickly made
Others take deep reflection
Don't jump to others' schedules
Take the time to be satisfied
This is not procrastination
Rather careful consideration
Don't let expediency overrule your intuition

Once the decision is made
Let it be
Don't try to second-guess
It may be right
It may be wrong
Only time will tell
Be prepared to change if experience proves it wrong
None of your decisions will change the world
Some may impact the course of your life
Remember they are in your control
You have made them
You can change them

DAWN

First light slowly extinguishes the stars in the sky
I stand, a solitary being, on the shore
Gazing across the emptiness of the sea
Nothing to be seen but a lonely gull
Winging its way in a lazy carefree circle
Carried by the same gentle warm breeze
That caresses my body like a gentle massage.
The sounds calm my many thoughts
The soft breaking roll of the small waves around my feet
Is like a symphony of repetitive sound
Leaving me in a state of suspended animation
Broken only by the sharp cry of the gull
As another joins its space.
My mind floats as if part of the sea
The sun emerges across the line between sea and sky.
Sunrays shimmer across the water
Dancing from wavelet to wavelet
Leaving behind a spreading orange glow
That makes the sky and sea seem like one.
Covered by a blanket of warm colour
Dawn has emerged from the sleep of night.
I take my first step into the warm sea of light
The water envelops my body
Taking the feeling of calm even deeper
I roll onto my back and float freely.
The sun continues its rise
The shimmering colour fades and disappears
The sea and sky are no longer one
The new day has begun.
I move slowly back to shore
To emerge with glistening droplets
Reflecting the sun from my body.
I am no longer alone
Others have found the beach
Too late to see and feel
The splendour of the dawning day.

SCAVENGERS OF DEATH

They spiral upwards in the currents
Their wings extended to catch each breath of air
Majestic birds of nature
Soaring from updraft to updraft
Swooping down with barely a hint of movement
Slow languid wings take them aloft once more
To find a perch
From which to view the landscape.
High upon the topmost branches of the stark dead elm they sit
These winged carnivores
Living upon the death of other creatures
Spotted while cruising the currents.

Close up upon landing
These guardians of the sky lose their majestic cloak
They fight each other for the carrion
Tearing it apart with sharp beaks
Their tattered feathers giving no hint of grace
Dark ugly creatures of your dreams
To be banished from your thoughts if not feared.
So ugly
Yet at times so beautiful
As they soar high
With a freedom unknown
By most creatures here on the earth.

BIRTHDAY CELEBRATION

Laughter fills the air
It's a time for rejoicing
Sharing with those gathered round
Celebrating the joy of 75 years of living
The things you've seen
The friends you've made
The family you've raised
The ones you've lost
All part and parcel of who you are

MORE THAN FRIENDS

The spark of passion ignites the space between them
The warm glow draws them into its embrace
Hands reach tentatively across the space
To gently caress the face and limbs of the other
Lips meet in a gentle searching way
Their hearts quicken
The warm glow becomes a fire
Lips aggressively respond
Fingers and hands frantically follow the contours of the other
Clothes fall away
Their bodies meld together in a full embrace
They ache with a burning desire
To become joined as one
Slowly as if to prolong the journey
They touch and probe
Until no longer able to wait
They become one
Rising through the pulsing contractions
To the inevitable release
Followed by the warm glow of being together
Of having shared themselves in their entirety

SUMMER CONFERENCE

Viewed through the conference window
The sunlight bounces off the shimmering surface of the lake
Drawing the eyes of those seated within
Shifting the focus from what the speaker is saying
He's doing his best to keep our interest
It's hard to compete with nature's beauty
Displayed in all its splendour
Close outside the windows

A LINE OF COLOUR

Reds, blues, greens
All the colours of the rainbow
Interspersed among the white
Wave in the summer breeze

They stretch in a taunt row from house to shed
Suspended from the line
Hung to dry in the warm sun
Spots of colour worn by those who dwell within

A family of four from what can be seen
A father's blue coveralls
His place of work patched on the chest
Fading from their frequent washing

A mother's favourite red dress
Obviously often hung there
Will smell and feel fresh
When next worn in her busy life

The children's colours are not as faded
A bright pink toddler's playsuit
A child's dark blue jeans and green shirt
Maroon pyjamas with splashes of yellow

They seem to dance as the breeze quickens
The line bounces from the weight
The garments clinging each to the other
Together like the family to which they belong

WHISPERS

She whispers quietly in her child's ear
Murmurings shared each night
Just before the lights go out
The stories read
The secrets of the day shared
Tears left over from sad events kissed away
The covers snuggled up
There's a quiet moment as her thoughts settle
She bends over to share one last word
Small arms encircle her neck
No more words are spoken
Love is in the air
The perfect way to drift into sleep
Secure in knowing that same love
Awaits you when you wake

PLACE OF DREAMS

The day is over
Night beckons
Sleep is but a heartbeat away
I cast my thoughts aside
I drift away
I enter the state of nothingness
The rhythm of my body slows
The reverie of dreams begins
Some are soothing, some are goofy
Some shock, some make me angry
Some break through to my consciousness
I awake with a start
Still out of breath from the chase
Still panicked from the fear
I'm safe; I'm in my bed
The dream fades
I drift off again
Returning to the place of dreams
Until morning calls

FROM DISCOVERY TO DISCOVERY

We wander through our time on earth
Often unsure of our destination
Living from moment to moment
Anticipating our next discovery.

We start our wandering as children
Holding the hands of those around us
Our boundaries set by those same hands
Our world expands, as we set out alone
Examining the things around us
Finding friends to join us in the exploration
Looking for things that intrigue us.
Our discoveries shape us as we grow
Our interests change
Our passions flourish
We become more focused as time moves on.
Our first job must use the talents we've acquired
If not we find another
Not willing to waste our time.
With love and family we put down roots
That makes it hard to wander far.
With our children the exploration quickens once again.
Sometimes, we must pause
To discover what lies within ourselves.
There is no path for the life we live
As we wander from discovery to discovery
Exploring wherein we dwell.

BEYOND COMFORT

It is easy to be too comfortable in your space
No surprises, no unexpected twists,
But alas no new challenges,
No whetting of your appetite for things unknown.
We need those new experiences to feel alive
We need to open doors that lead to unfamiliar places
We need new friends to broaden our connections
We need to feel fresh for the day ahead
The doldrums of comfortability will suck out our juice for living.
Time does not stand still
Open the doors
Explore what lies beyond
You'll feel refreshed each day you awake.

FROM THE FRONT PORCH

From the front porch I look out
On a small part of the world around me.
The hammock beneath me lethargically moves to and fro
A warm breeze sweeps intermittently across my face
The leaves in the maple rustle with each breath of air
Roses, petunias, marigolds display their splash of colour
In the boxes, baskets, and gardens so carefully planted and tended
By the person sharing this relaxing place with me.

The colours of green are everywhere I look
The deep dark hue of the maple
The lighter willowy green of new growth alfalfa
The yellow mellow green of the soyabeans
Struggling to establish themselves for the frantic growth of summer
The richness of the conifers in their solitary line along the fencerow
All the greens of early summer
Before the heat and drought blanch them out.

SUMMER SNOWSTORM

It's a warm dry day of early summer
The air is clear with a hint of more heat to come
The sun has no clouds to deflect its glare
Dust swirls dance across the yard.
A snowstorm of poplar seeds swirls by
Set free by the warm breeze brushing past me.
Each with their own parachute of cotton fluff
Floating on the currents of air to whatever their destination
Far across the fields for many, close by for others.
They matt the screen doors of the house blocking the fresh breeze
They form a carpet of white on the green lawn
They cling to the cat's whiskers and to my eyelashes
They cluster the size of footballs in the sheltered corners.
Millions of seeds from a single tree
The fertility of nature floating past my eyes
Determined to grow again.

FROM THE FARMHOUSE PORCH

Listen to what I hear this summer day
Sounds layered one upon the other
The breeze echoing past my ear
The angry buzz of a bee
The rustle of maple leaves as the wind picks up
The almost sighs of poplar leaves one against the other
The random chorus of sparrows, finches, doves
The swish of passing cars
The hum of a lone motorbike seeking company for the day
The roar of motorcycles driven by grandparents in search of youth
Cows calling to each other with deep bellows as if haunted
The drone of barn exhaust fans keeping the air fresh
The rumble of the train, whistling at every crossing
The anxious sputter of an ultralight flying overhead
The beating of my own heart resonating deep within me
The sounds of life
Anxious to be heard

MORTALITY

Hardly a week passes
Without man's mortality slapping me in the face.
A unique time period of tragedy
Occurring all too frequently to ones you know.
A friend's son fell from the sky
While cruising the sunset in an ultralight.
A neighbour's brother and a childhood acquaintance
Unexpectantly is no longer here among us.
Overnight a happy faced baby, the focus of her parents' lives,
Faces a grim battle with leukaemia raging through her body.

I wonder what the next week will bring
To the lives that I know
Will there be joy?
Will there be sadness?
One never knows
But this I do know
There are multitudes of days of joy for living
For every day of sadness felt.

RELEASED

The pencil is poised
Waiting for the words to appear
From the place within me
That creates the unexpected.
Thoughts that paint pictures in the mind
Words that find connection in the mundane
Phrases that capture a fleeting feeling
Poems that leap onto the page.

Once released the words rush to the paper
Impatient for the pencil to move quicker
Before even a single syllable is lost.
A tap to my spirit has been opened
Images are being painted with words
The colours can be seen
The sounds can be heard
The emotion can be felt
The desire to share these surprising insights
Into how I see our world
Is as impatient as the flow of words itself.

THE HEAT OF SUMMER

It's been a warm sultry night
The sheets stuck like jelly
Opening my eyes is a slow heavy struggle
Yesterday's heat still fills the room
I shuffle down the stairs
My body in a languid steamy daze
I open the outside door to sniff for a sign of refreshing air
Not a whisper of breeze greets me
The sun is enveloped in a diffuse haze
Holding the earth in its breath-stealing grasp
Another day of close enveloping heat waits
I impatiently yearn for that next cool breeze

THE SILVER POPLAR

For a hundred years it has stood there
Planted by those who built this house
A single silver poplar casting its shade
On those within its reach

A mighty tree nearing the end of its life
Its knurled bark touched by generations of hands
Several bare dead branches extend beyond the greenery
A reminder of the fate of all things in nature

Birds call from its branches
A family of squirrels has made it home
It howls with delight when strong winds bend its limbs
Shedding the dead debris that clutters its space

A swing that my daughters used still clings to its branch
Many peels of laughter emanated from that spot in days pass
It hangs there still, a reminder of fond memories
A spot for visiting children to test their wings

An elliptical rock sits stoically at its base
A kettle transported to this spot by my grandfather
Many a child has sat upon that rock waiting for the swing
Or simply enjoying the shade of the friendly tree

The poplar will not be there forever
But for now it remains
A solitary reminder of the history
It has seen pass beneath its branches

THE ROAD TO WHERE

What journey are they on today?
The people in the cars passing down my road.
Some flash by with total concentration on their destination,
Others meander along looking this way and that
Oblivious to the line forming behind them
Unmindful of the flaring tempers of those looking for a gap
To leap into and accelerate on their way.
Some are cautiously pulling a trailer
Their first trip with something more than a car or truck
An otherwise leisurely drive turned into a chore
As they search for that spot of ground to pause for the night.
A temporary home away from home.

We are a transient society
Not content to be at home
We travel down many roads like this
Always on the move
To find a new friend
To visit friends from the past
To re-affirm family ties
To search out new places, new sights, new sounds
To see what lies beyond the next curve or hill
Searching for the next spot to pause awhile and catch our breath.
These journeys take up much of the life we live
Do we meander enough and enjoy the sights?
Are we too impatient to take the more leisurely route?
The pauses are what will be remembered
The time with friends and family
The places explored and lived within
The time spent enjoying the companionship of those you love.

Not many who have passed down the road today
Have taken that pause
To relish the world around them
They're in too much hurry
To get where they think they're going.

SMELLS OF SUMMER

The smells of summer are all around us
Some subtly weave themselves into the gentle breeze
Some are backgrounds to my memories
Some are suddenly there and just as suddenly gone
A tantalizing whiff of the familiar and unfamiliar
What are these smells?
The deep-rooted smell of dark earth, cultivated, ready for planting
The fresh aroma of newly cut alfalfa
The mature smell of hay as it passes through the baler
Too often the dark, mouldy odour of hay rotted by too many rains
The lingering, nostril filling smell of cows and calves
As you walk among them in the sweltering heat
The scent of wildflowers inhabiting the meadow
The smell of hard worked bodies of those who toil in summer jobs
The hint of diesel from the tractors working the land
The sneeze of pollen tickling your nose
All the smells of summer
Too often overcome
By the all-consuming powerful stench
Of liquid animal waste spread upon the ground
An attack against the senses
Till now lulled by the other smells of summer

READING

A good book
Impossible to define
Except by those who read it
Some read for entertainment
Some for enlightenment
Some for escape
Some to simply pass the time away
What's excitement for one is boredom for another
What enlightens one baffles another
What generates connection for some, seems senseless to others
One opens each new book with hopeful anticipation
We may be thrilled
We may be disappointed
Such is the joy of reading

A STATE OF NOTHINGNESS

My mind floats in a lethargic mist
of calm and relaxation
away from the frantic pace of everyday life.
An opportunity to renew my senses
to find that place of tranquillity
where to be alone with myself is enough.
Random gentle thoughts drift to the surface
then float effortlessly away.
The music of summer plays in the background.
A warm breeze playfully brushes over my body
causing the hair to move like mini masseuses
making my skin feel alive.
Languid smells permeate the heat around me
I try to identify each but find it impossible
to separate out their complexity.
I imagine the feel of chilled water
rushing down my throat
replenishing my body.
I am in a state of nothingness.
My senses are alive.

ALONE WITHIN OURSELVES

No matter the people we know or the places we've been
We spend most of our lives alone
We may share part of ourselves with those around us
We cannot share all of who we are
Our thoughts and feelings change too quickly
Only we know what has passed through our minds today
What emotions tugged at our heartstrings or cooled our passions
What snippets of memory have influenced our thinking
We are unique
We are often alone within ourselves
It makes us who we are

BARN FIRE

With a sudden explosion
the barn was enveloped in flames
Beyond control the fire raged
The squeals of terror from the sows trapped within
haunted those who heard
With sweat dripping effort the firemen saved the adjoining barn
Truckload after truckload of water was pumped into the flames
The structure quickly collapsed upon itself
Onlookers appeared
Some to move equipment
Some to reconnect electricity
Some to comfort the family
Some to simply offer whatever help they could
Others to watch and be silently glad it wasn't them facing this loss

The family had looks of distress on their faces
Their eyes filled with tears as the adrenaline rush passed
Each became another onlooker
Watching the men fight the flames with determination and purpose
despite the heat trapped within their protective gear

All that is left today is a pile of smoking ruins
to be cleared away and buried out of sight
A barn that withstood the elements for a century or more
gone in fiery hour of heat and smoke
What will rise in its place is unknown
A decision the family must soon face
For now it is enough to let the shock settle
and rejoice that each one of them is safe

FEAR OF CHANGE

Fear of change is more complex and stressful than change itself
Caught up in the future, the mind refuses to dwell in the present
It focuses incessantly on all the possible hidden outcomes
No opportunities only potential pitfalls are anticipated
The negatives blind your mind's eye
to the light of joy that change can bring
The fear becomes a physical feeling
The adrenalin rushes make you feel the fear

You seem possessed by emotion gnawing at your gut
The fear is real; almost tangible it attacks your body so
How does one assuage this fear?
Recognize it for what it is
Embrace the emotions so well hidden
There is no assurance of what the future will be
Only the opportunity for choices in the present
Do not fear what lies ahead
Examine it
The fear will subside
It has ensured that you do not rush unprepared into the future
Now let it go
Let your mind be at peace
Fear of future must not hold your spirit in check
It must be free to roam
To live the present to its fullest

SUMMER HEAT

Each passing day the corn and soyabeans struggle to survive
The lawns turn brown
The poplar leaves yellow and begin to fall
Dust swirls across the landscape
The drought and heat holds us tightly in its grasp
Refusing to loosen its stranglehold
Storms appear on the horizon with much sound and light
But pass us by with not a drop of rain
Anticipation of relief left unfulfilled
The nights are sultry, unbearable for sleeping
We awake each morning dull-witted
With little vigour for the day ahead
Tempers flare
The sun incessantly beats down
Enveloping each of us in an envelope of close air
Lethargy invades our being
The summer heat wave rolls on and on and on

DROPS OF LIFE

Once again the storm threatened to pass us by
Suddenly a shift in the wind drives it menacingly in our direction
The black clouds swirl and roll tumultuously one upon the other
Lightening leaps between cloud and earth
Shattering the black canvas of cloud and distant rain
A sizzle and crack resonate simultaneously
The wind picks up momentum
Tree limbs bend with the force
The first drops of rain ricochet off the windows
A curtain of rain whips across the fields towards us
Drowning us in a heavy downpour
The parched earth sucks the moisture in like a giant sponge
The drought stricken plants begin their renewal
As the roots feel the first rivulets of life reach their tentacles
A collective sigh can be felt
As man, plant and beast relish the relief from the sky
The drought has been broken
Nature once again has revitalized itself

SWALLOWS GATHER

The swallows are gathering
They perch soldier-like along the hydro line
Close by the house and lawn
Overlooking the bug filled alfalfa field verdant from the recent rains
They swoop and dive on practiced wing
Harvesting a meal
They flash by, changing direction on the fly
Just inches from the ground
Returning to their perch
To preen, groom, and chatter
A sudden breeze startles them from their place
They are like a wave of fluttering wings
Riding the current above the field
Turning as one to once again settle all in line
Until now, this season, they've been solitary pairs
Raising this year's crop of hatchlings
Now they gather as a flock
To build a camaraderie
To last them on their long migration

THE FLOWER GARDEN

The gardens are awash with colour
Reds, greens and blues
Interspersed with every other imaginable hue
A canvas painted by nature
Tended by one who loves to see her work bloom
Careful planting, mixing, matching
Ensures a summer long flowering
Secret potions to encourage them to be the best
A splash of colour circling the house
Part of what makes it home

104

THE SHELL

My body is but a shell wherein I dwell
It is no part of the essence of who I am
All that I am truly lives within my spirit
My intellect, my emotions are what defines me
My body gives my spirit voice
It provides a physical presence for others to see and hear
It takes me to new spaces and places
So the true part of me may learn and grow
It allows me to procreate
So one of the next generation of spirits may dwell therein
I will live but a short time in the continuum of time
But the spirit within may live forever
In the hearts and minds of those who follow

LEAVING HOME

This house has been my home for my entire life
I was born and reared here and my father before me
I've spent most of my adult life living in this space
Our daughters were conceived and grew up within these walls
They played in the yard
They walked the lane
They knew the animals that were in the barn
Their cats and dogs were here to greet them each morning
All that is changing
The girls are moving on
We're moving away
Away from what has been home
To a new place that will become home
This place will be here to visit
To pass a few days or perhaps a week
It will change, we will change
How long before someone else lives here is unknown
It's not easy to leave a home
A place of familiarity, a place of memories, a place of family
A place that has been one of the anchors of my life
But it's time for change
A new place, a new style of living
Will it be right for us?
Time will tell

A NEW JOB BECKONS

A new job beckons me
I'm ready to try something new yet familiar
I need the new challenge
I need to feel the juices flow
It has taken a long time to be ready
To put the old job behind me
Not easy to do because it had become a part of me
A part that I was ill prepared to give up
It took time to let it go
There is no space here on the farm for me
No sense of engagement, no sense of accomplishment
I need people, the interaction
The engagement of doing a job that needs doing
My mind needs fodder for my imagination to wander
So I can practice the new attitude for living that I am learning
To be in the present
To leave my responsibility at the door
To take time to feel my emotional self
To write about the things I see and feel
None of them easy for me to do without some trepidation
This is a new chapter in our book of life
Together, my spouse and I, begin this journey
New job, new home, new beginning

UNTITLED

She's uncertain of her path in life
Which direction should she go?
She loved the cows but now they're gone
Home has changed
It's not the place she knew
The camaraderie of working there
With friends and family is no more
University challenged her mettle
She's not sure it leads where she wants to go
But the friends she made there add a sparkle to her life
It's now even more a struggle
As mom and dad are moving
She may not know it but they also fear
This unsettling time in their lives
Together the family will prevail
The paths they're on will be more clear
As they share this uncertain time together

A NEW WISDOM

The world is a cauldron of turmoil
Petty squabbles, racial wars, starving children
Jealousy, hatred, anger are all too often the common thread
Joy, happiness, love are seldom found on the world stage
Is it a basic human imperfection that creates this kind of world?
A flaw that no amount of intellect and reason can overcome
Are we destined to be a people without true compassion
For those who dwell on this small planet?
Power is such an aphrodisiac
It corrupts and blinds those who lead?
Aggression is oft championed in the name of some supreme being
Spouting a religious doctrine justifying war and terror.
There is no such god or deity
Only the weakness of human nature
Twisting our human frailties.

I fear for our future unless a new wisdom prevails
A wisdom that can look beyond our history
A wisdom that takes us to a new consciousness
A wisdom that encourages peace and human understanding.

AN EASY JOB

It's an easy job or so we thought
To remove wallpaper from the rooms
It'll be ready for painting quick as a flash
Assemble the tools
Sponge, water, stripper, scrappers
Ready to begin
Start with the dinosaur paper in the smallest room
Grip the corner and pull
The vinyl will peel off like a skin off a banana
No such luck!
It rips into long shreds
Leaving behind as much as came off
Water, of course, will not penetrate the outer layer
Wet, scrape, wet, scrape
On and on and on it goes
By the end of the afternoon we stop
Discouraged, ill tempered, unable to face another wall
We leave to return another day with patience hopefully restored

Many phone calls to seek advice
Use vinegar, use fabric softener
It'll be a snap
With trepidation we return
It works!
One, two three rooms done in a day
This is easy, no problems now
One more room to finish
One hour at the most!
Wet it down and begin to scrape
What did they use?
Crazy glue to spite the next owners
Spray, scrape, spray, scrape
Scrape, scrape, scrape
Finally it's done
Hours have passed
We'll never paper in our lives
Now on to the painting
Quick as a flash.........

110

DUSK

The sun is setting
Long shadows stretch across the lawn
Stillness settles on the landscape
Broken by the jumbled sounds of the many and varied insects
Hidden in the grass, trees, and fields
Calling each to the other or simply marking their spot.
The loud call of the cicada moth rising above all others
The crickets providing the background harmony
A train whistle calls hauntingly across the distance
Tiny moths float by on the breath of a breeze
The faint rustle of leaves adds to the languid feeling
The shadows continue to lengthen.
A single tree's outline now stretches to the fence line
The air is increasingly tinged with a touch of dampness
The birds are settling on their perches
Their calls much muted from the peak of day
The sun brushes the tree line on the horizon.
With no clouds to paint red and orange hues
It will go down in a singular blaze of glory.
The shadows are merging together
The music of the evening plays on
A fleeting dusk has arrived

WAITING

We spend much of our life waiting
Waiting in line
Waiting for an appointment
Waiting for a phone call
We fill the time with needless dithering
Or simply let frustration build
It is not easy to remain calm while one waits
Think of the wait as a pause in your busy life
Use the time to let your mind wander
Read a book
Write a letter to a friend
Cherish the calmness
Think not of what you next must do
Be in the moment of waiting
An unplanned opportunity to be absolutely grounded in the present
Accept it
The wait will more quickly pass
Too soon your frantic life will resume
With little time for such a breath of calm

FLIGHT

The door is closed
Ready for take-off
Strangers all
We sit rigidly in our assigned seats
Anticipating the power of acceleration
None of us comfortable to be in this confined space
Our lives in the hands of man and machine
The safety video fuels our imagination
Conversation stops as the plane begins to roll
We hold our collective breath as the point of rotation is reached
The wheels leave the runway
Settle in the belly with a groan and thud
We're airborne
The tension eases but does not dissipate
Conversations resume
Heads bob as the plane dips through air pockets
This is not a natural place to be
Above the space that birds fly
Few herein will feel at ease
Until once again we touch the earth

CROSS-EXAMINATION

A welcoming atmosphere of forced camaraderie
As the opposing sides take their places
Aligned across the boardroom table
An expanse that defines the gulf between their views

The affidavits have been filed
The time for cross-examination has arrived
The lawyers pose their carefully crafted questions
The respondents listen for a hidden trap of words

A verbatim transcript is being recorded
To be later copied and perused
To find that comment or interpretation
To give credence to a final argument

A decision will someday be rendered
One side will win, the other lose
The winner will feel relieved and pleased
The loser much chagrined

Such is the path
When common sense and compromise fail
To find solutions to satisfy each side
Outside the court of law

THE PATH OF LIFE

We walk our path of life but once from beginning to end
There is no predicting what lies beyond the bend.
No matter the unexpected turns or tragedies we encounter
We cannot retrace our steps towards eternity.
Each path is unique
Waiting to unfold as we move through our lives.
With tentative steps we begin our life's journey
Our stride lengthens and grows more confident.

We may falter sometimes along the way but never leave the path
We join hands with others whose paths join ours for a while
Often our paths will suddenly diverge, never to cross again.
Even the path of our spouse will only run parallel to ours for a time
Our paths will never merge to become one.
We start our children down their own path of life
We cannot ensure their path will be without conflict
We can only teach them what they'll need to climb the tricky parts

There is much to see along our path
If we take the time to hear the sounds
Feel the breath of life
Bask in the joys
Transcend the sad stretches.
We may tire and our feet begin to shuffle
But without fail, each day we live
The journey never ends.

QUIET PLACE

I am in a quiet room devoid of outside sounds
The quiet surrounds me with its emptiness
No sound of wind against the windowpane
No birds chirping in the branches
No rustling of maple leaves
No echo of cars passing on the road
An eerie quietness after all the sounds of summer
Heard constantly from our front porch.

What can I hear?
Household sounds
Water running, doors squeaking, kitchen activities
A faint ringing in my ears
The sound of blood rushing through my body
The sound of my pencil moving across this paper
All sounds of living.
Not the sounds of nature
To soothe a part of me
Yearning for a connection to the world I live within.

THE EMPTY SHELVES

The shelves are barren
The books are packed, ready for the move
Books that have been an important part of our lives
Books that taught us many things
Books that entertained through words and pictures
Books to reference all manner of pressing questions
Books to re-assure us
Dictionaries, poetry, biographies
A history of our community and home
A multitude of children's books, most often read at bedtime
Diaries lovingly recording the details of our lives
All these books have filled the shelves
A treasured part of home
Soon to be once again displayed
In another house about to become our home

BOXES

Boxes, boxes everywhere
Filled with our things and some from those who went before us
The shelves are bare
The cupboards empty
Everything is packed
Ready for the move
All shapes and sizes, the boxes are stacked in each room
The contents noted, the destination indicated
The clutter of our lives in boxes destined for basement storage
Like all our friends, we hold onto things
To mark the events of our lives
Or stir memories of nostalgic family ties
We've become connoisseurs of cardboard these last few weeks
We scoured the neighbourhood stores
Looking for boxes strong enough
To trust with all that we possess

THE BOUQUET

Our children often surprise us
With glimpses of an inner self we seldom know
But an important part of who they are
She portrays herself as impatient with nostalgia
No time for romantic stirrings
How surprised I was to see appear
A bouquet created from dried roses
Hung in her room for several years
Roses I gave her on her sixteenth birthday
Roses from a friend for a surprise valentine
Grouped together now
In a visual reminder of her past

MOVING DAY

One week has passed since the move began
The truck was loaded with little fuss
The house I called home for most of my life
Stood empty, still and cold
A scattering of furniture in a few rooms
Now a place to perhaps visit but not to dwell within
As we drove away a part of me felt empty
I was leaving the place
Where I grew up
Where I returned having been away
Where I worked and played
Where we raised our children
Where we have shared our lives for so many years
Where I was loved and loved in return
My place of refuge
The home of my heart and soul

THE NEW PLACE

We are here
A new place to call home
Starting to feel familiar but not yet settled
Boxes still to unpack, furniture to buy, pictures to hang
A semblance of order slowly emerging
My favourite chair has found its spot
The cat is cautiously exploring her new territory
I think I know which cupboard the glasses are in
The sounds of the house no longer surprise me
Light switches can be found in the dark
The grass has been cut for the first time
Flowerbeds are being planned
The local library has been scouted
Routines are emerging
Now what is my telephone number?

I AM WHO I AM

A new job is about to begin
A feeling of trepidation is slowly taking hold.
It's been awhile since I've had a routine
Of responsibility and expectation of results.
I need to take each day one at a time
Realize the first few weeks are
For meeting people
For being briefed
For understanding the dynamics of the issues.
There is no need to shoulder the problems of the industry
Issues and challenges will always be there
There will be no magic wand to wave.
Working with the people involved
Understanding their perspectives
Challenging them to look for innovative solutions
That will be my goal.
I am there to facilitate, to encourage, to listen
I need to keep my perspective and be myself
I am who I am
I am not what others expect.

THE END OF DAY

I'm tired
It's been a full and satisfying day
I'm sitting here alone
Away from the television noise
Relaxing in a favourite chair
Letting the languid feeling flow through my body
My head rests on my hand
My feet and hands throb
With the sensation of exhausted expectation
My mind and body yearn for a deep nourishing sleep
To vanquish the fog from my brain
To reenergize my body for tomorrow's adventures
To reconnect my mind, body and spirit
Such is the end of a good day

THE FIRST DAY

About to begin
New job, new challenges
People to meet, policies to know
Politics to understand
Personalities to unravel
All part of a new experience
To be lived to its fullest
Not one to be fixated on
Not one to trigger my over responsibility
But rather to be kept in balance
With all the parts of my life
Neither my intellect nor emotions can run rough shod
I approach the day with a sense of calm
Practicing what I've learned about myself
This job will be only a part of my life

THE FIRST WEEK

The nights are long
A new bed, a new job, a new routine
All conspire to prevent a deep sleep
I awake rested but not fully alert
My mind could easily focus on the lack of sleep
If allowed it could swirl out of control
But I remind myself to take each day one at a time
I need to write this down
I need to read a book
I need to focus outside the place I'm in
The job feels comfortable
The people are welcoming
It is a new routine that requires acceptance
It's been two years since I've done these things
Balance and focus is what I need
It will come with time
I must be patient
I am learning to live a new way
I should not be surprised it is not easy
I know it can be achieved

THANKSGIVING WALK

The sun is breaking above the horizon
Its rays in flight across the landscape.
There's a hint of frost in the air
Each breath is crisp and clean
It's a glorious time to walk down the lane.
Newly planted wheat is sprouting up
Soon to be a lush mat of green
A sharp contrast to the browns, yellows, and flashes of orange
Which mark the individual trees along the fence line.
No sounds from songbirds to break the morning silence
But rather sharp brittle cries
Emanating from a flock of starlings
Undulating just above the treetops.
High overhead migrating geese cleave the sky
Too far away to be heard.
Fall has arrived!
Nature is preparing for its long winter sleep
Tired from its seasons of birth, growth, and harvest
Ready to rest and gather strength for the seasons ahead.
A feeling of cool sharpness cuts through the air
It wakes my senses
To the crispness of the moment

TIME REVISITED

Time is relentless as we count off the minutes of our lives
At birth, the time ahead seems endless
At death, our time has been but a moment in the continuum.
Few of us can live our lives without regard for time
We measure much of what we do by time
What age did we learn to walk?
What time do we wake up?
How many years did we go to school?
How long have we had this job?
How long has our marriage lasted?
Birthdays, anniversaries are celebrated
As if the simple passage of time is an accomplishment.
Time has become a focus over which there is no control.
What if each moment was filled with being the most we can be
Without regard for the moment in time?
Our lives would flow from one experience to another
Filling the space of our lives with memories
Uncluttered by the marking of time
A rich cornucopia of experience to be cherished
And shared with those important to our lives.

THE FIRE WITHIN

A smouldering fire burns within me
waiting for a breath of opportunity to fan it to flame
An opportunity to put into words
the thoughts colliding one upon the other within my psyche
seeking an emotional thread to bind them together
I know not the source of this hidden fire
but often feel its heat permeate my being
It sucks the juices from my inner core
until with a sudden burst of energy the thoughts meld together
as intellect and emotion become entwined
They begin to flow and form the words that here appear
The fire dies down
The embers glow faintly
Patiently waiting for the next breath of opportunity
to flame forth with words gleaned
from some spot deep within my soul

ON THE CREST

I stand alone.
A solitary figure on the crest of the hill
Gazing across the expanse of farmland stretching out before me.
The neat symmetrical squares of yellow and green
Interspersed with warm dark fog shrouded patches
Of newly turned soil.
Fiery rays of orange precede the slowly emerging sun.
Fall has arrived
Harvest is nearly over
The landscape is beginning its transformation to winter's solitude.
A solitude that will permeate deep within my soul
To touch my heart and at times
Bring a certain melancholy to my thoughts.
The seasons of frenetic activity are passing
The time for peering wordlessly
Into a warm blazing fire in the hearth approaches.
My footprints will soon mark my way on the snow-covered paths
Winding through the eerily quiet forest floor.
Each breath will be sharp and clean
My fingers will tingle with the cold
My face will shine with a red glow from the bite of a winter wind.
The long nights and the day's deep shadows
Will conspire to dampen my energy
As if a part of me is hibernating,
Waiting for the exhilaration of spring.
For now I stand alone
Basking in the spreading sunlight
Feeling totally alive
An integral part of the world around me.
My next step will break this kaleidoscope of thought
I will emerge from this solitary moment
With a feeling of peace and reverence
For the awesome glory of nature's landscape.

ALONE WITHIN THE CROWD

I sit alone
surrounded by the crowd
here but not here
alive but not alive to the sounds around me
so intensely focused on myself
those around me do not exist
I am suspended in time
searching for a way
to paint the images that are flashing through my mental reverie
Slowly the phrases begin to emerge
a thread of cohesive thought and emotion begins to form
Suddenly a torrent of words captures the moment
to be later recalled and committed to paper
I have found that which was eluding me
I can now rejoin those around me
Few have noticed that I had left them
Those that did acknowledge my return with a faint smile
for they too escape at times within themselves
to find a momentary quiet spot
alone with their own thoughts
away from the noise and angst of the crowd

SHARING?

Two friends meet to share their lives
Their hopes, their dreams, their expectations
If close enough, their fears, their disappointments, their lost loves
But alas there is no depth of feeling
No tremble to their voices
No joyous bubbling of their laughter
No sight of tears, no touch of hands
No sense of emotional energy passing between them
For they have met in cyberspace
Their words carefully chosen and appearing on the screen
No chance for intimate whispers of support in such a public place
A meeting, an exchange of words
But no passion, no true connection

CONCERT TIME

The pace quickens, then slows into a melancholy pause
A crescendo builds and then bursts through
I have become a part of the music
As if my heart is beating out the time
Every part of me is possessed
By the sound filling the hushed space
I'm floating just above the notes
Suspended on a wave of emotion released by the sensory attack
I can feel the sound beating against my body
I can see the fluid movement of musicians and instruments
A simultaneous physical and sensory integration of sound
All my thoughts are suspended
The transformation is complete
I am one with the music

WARMTH OF SELF

We weave a complicated pattern of thoughts to define who we are
Like a quilt made from scraps
Thoughts alone mean nothing but sewn together become a whole
Like a warm blanket on a cold night
Our definition of self gives us comfort and solace

In the living of our everyday lives
We must often wrap that blanket around ourselves
Or risk losing our place amongst the turmoil

Warmth of self gives us the confidence
To face the challenges
To mine the opportunities
To balance the tragedies
To face each day with celebration

We must keep our blanket within reach
No matter who tries to take it
We have created this warmth
We must not let the cold of self-doubt get through the fibres
We have spent a lifetime weaving together

OPPORTUNITY LOST

The rapid pace of our lives dampens our sensibilities
Opportunities are missed to express our love
To spouse, to children, to parents, to friends
We seem to have so little time to share our feelings
We convince ourselves there is no time today
Tomorrow will be soon enough
But alas, tomorrows are sometimes stolen from us
A person who means so much to us is no longer there
Suddenly gone
Too late to show our love
Too late to spend the time to share our lives
The opportunity missed has become an opportunity lost forever
No second chances when death intervenes
We feel regret and sorrow to have squandered the chance
To fill the brief pauses in our lives
With a warm word, a gentle touch, an intimate conversation
All simple expressions of love
To those who mean so much to us
That will mean more at life's end
Than all the frantic activity that filled our daily lives

TENSION

The tension hangs suspended in the space between them
Spoken words mask the true emotions that are achingly contained
His eyes no longer dance as she speaks
She no longer can sense how he feels
Their busy lives have become focused beyond themselves
Are they losing their lives together?
Or is it the next step in an evolving relationship
Between a man and a woman
Joined in marriage
Loved by the children they've raised
Struggling to live the autumn of their lives
Wondering what might have been
If different choices had been made

129

THINGS

Things, things and more things
We all possess things that fill the space of our lives
They clutter our homes
Line our garage
Overflow the trunk of the car
We spend hours shopping for more
Gadgets that promise to simplify small tasks
Junk that others have cast away but hold promise for us
Tools we might use some rainy day
Another blue sweater
A great new tie
Magazines, books full of the trivia of life
All items to add to what we already possess

Possessions define too much of who we are
Our need to create an image for others to see
Our need to acquire material things
To fill a life that feels empty
But things will not fill the void
The day will come when, too late, we realize
Love, friendship and empathy for our fellow man
Are the things to soothe our spirit
And truly fill the empty space of our lives

BRIEF GLIMPSES

I wander this earth
Searching for the magic
To fill my spirit with certainty
To feel alive, to feel serene
With all that I do and feel

———————o———————

Within any crowd, a quiet spot exists
I often seek it out
A spot to give me respite
From loud voices and forced camaraderie
A place from which I observe
The swirling of the crowd, the passion of the faces
I can feel the energy of human contact
Pulsating with the ebb and flow of conversation
Without these momentary escapes
I would be left gasping for air
Suffocated by the closeness of the crowd

———————o———————

Where does the music take me?
Outside of myself to some other place
My mind floats upon the melody
I feel each note touch my heartstrings
The fullness of the sound floods my breast
I breathe the energy of the moment
It sets me alive with passionate feeling
I am living the sound
It fills the room to overflowing
My senses merge to one
The music is within me

FAMILY GATHERING

The room is filled with the joy of laughter
The family has gathered to celebrate the holiday

Together they will share a meal,
              their memories,
                          their tales of where they've been
A common bond draws them to this day

They have shared their lives,
              their accomplishments,
                          their disappointments
Together they grew into adults

They left to pursue their dreams
The security of memories past playing
As the music in the background of their lives

Today is a gift of love
Recalling the emotional ties of the past
Testing the possibility of new pursuits
Secure in the knowledge that come what may
The bond of family will be there
An uncompromising source of support

The hours pass
Quiet intimate conversations replace the laughter
Deeper connections are being made
Each has grown since they last met
There are new nuances of character to reveal
The family has changed yet remained the same

The day draws to a close
Goodbyes are loud and long
They linger at the door
Unwilling to leave the warmth

CRISIS

The air crackles with tension
Each person is on the edge of his chair
Trying to avoid a word or phrase
That would be the spark
To explode the meeting into anger and confrontation
A crisis has brought them here
Who is to blame?
Who will shoulder the responsibility?
Are fingers going to be pointed?

The opening remarks are a dance of unsure posturing
One brave trembling voice acknowledges an error on his part
Suddenly the tension eases
Others admit their complicity
Questions to gain an understanding are posed
The mood has shifted
Together the solution can be found.

REBELLION

A quiet whisper of discontent breathes across the countryside
They have lived too long without hope
They meet together despairing for their children's future
Their muffled whispers grow into loud voices of anger
"We will no longer live like this"
"We must rid ourselves of the tyrant"
"Who will lead us?"
Sudden silence hushes the crowded room
They cast their eyes about the group
Searching for one who can take their anger into action
Is their not one of them prepared to take the risk?

One voice rises above the silence
With trembling words a leader emerges
One, who till now, has remained silent
She wept alone when her only son died from illness
Her husband's death in the conscripted army
Brought a tear to her heart
She can no longer be still
Her words gather strength and fan the embers of discontent
From out of her silent suffering a cry for freedom erupts
Her words excite the room
The weak of heart find unexpected purpose in their miserable lives
The word spreads rapidly from village to village
She rallies those around her and kindles a fierce loyalty
She will lead them, she will not falter
With that one clear voice, the flames of rebellion are lit

WRITER'S BLOCK

No substance to the thoughts
No connection to the words
My mind is locked
I search for the key
To unleash the flow of words
Will it be a simple phrase, a sound, a mental image
To free that which is held within?

MEMORY SOUNDS

The flames effortlessly dance in the fireplace
A blanket of peace and quiet warms my being
A glowing image of tranquility soothes my senses
My ear is attuned to the faintest sound in the memory of my mind

What will be the first sound to break through?
  The haunting call of a morning dove at first light
  The music of rippling water brushing past the rocks in the stream
  The joyful sound of laughter from children at play
  The wrenching cry of one who has lost their way
All these sounds and multitudes more are stored deep in my mind
Waiting to be played in these brief pauses in my busy life

The first sound I hear is not a random choice
Rather, my inner voice is whispering to me
Seeking to free the emotion that is sheltered just below the surface
Anxious to break through my calm façade
The first sound I hear mirrors that feeling
It may be joy, it may be sadness, it may be anger
Each a part of the harmony of my life

IF ONLY IT WERE SO!

Rush, rush, rush!
Never pause to listen, to feel at ease.
Busy, busy, busy!
Never rest.
Work, work, work!
Never take a break.
Bitch, bitch, bitch!
Never satisfied with our place.
Want, want, want!
Never content with what we have.

—— how much more fulfilling our lives would be if we were ——

To listen carefully to those around us before rushing off
  To pause to find moments of quiet during our busy days
    To find pleasure in our work and intersperse it with play
      To rejoice in our lives and in the lives of others
        To be content with our possessions and be willing to share

If only it were so!

LOOK INTO THEIR EYES

Their eyes reflect the lives they've lived till now
A veil of pain clouds their vision
No hope for tomorrow
This day may be their last
Their bodies wasted from hunger
Their memories overwhelmed by fear
No families to love them
These orphans of war wander aimlessly
Abandoned by a world not of their making
A world that has shut its own eyes to this travesty of hopelessness

WHISPERS

Loud voices, brittle and raw,
Shout above the din of our everyday lives.
No one listens!
Our ear is attuned to catch the whispers
—— the intimate human message destined only for us alone.

Whispers of love strengthens the bond of mother and infant
   Whispers of support send a child confidently into the world
      Whispers of love bridge the gap between long distance lovers
       Whispers of passion send tingles up their spines

Whispers of distrust tears two lives apart
   Whispers of uncertainty give us cause for angst
      Whispers of anger turn friends into enemies
       Whispers of bitterness spoil us for life

Whispers about others become malignant rumours
   Whispers of intolerance build a nation of bigots
      Whispers of immorality destroys our confidence in leadership
         Whispers of discontent fan the flames of rebellion

All these whispers from one to another
—— muted messages in the clatter of our world ——
Are heard clearly above the loud voices that shatter the silence.

NIGHT

Lingering shadows steal stealthily across the landscape
The sun sinks lower and lower into its sea of colour
The dust of day hangs in the air
The subdued chatter of birds signals the pass of day
The unbroken shadow of night arrives
No moon to cast its false sense of light
A hint of dampness cleanses the air as the dust settles to earth
The cricket chorus warms to its repetitive symphony
A discerning eye catches the swooping dive of bats in flight
Fireflies dance across the lawn
The sentinels of the night hoot from their perches
The cacophony of day has been banished
Calmness claims this spot of nature
We settle into our beds
To rest, to be renewed
For the next day in our busy lives.

WINDY

The wind howls across the open prairie
A dusting of wind-borne snow sifts through the doors
The windlass high overhead creaks and groans
The windmill in the yard spins uncontrollably.
On the windward side of the grain elevator the old men huddle
around the stove
Their windbreakers pulled up around their ears
Ignoring the windchill just beyond the circle of warmth.
A look of boredom on their faces as the oldest windbag among them
Tells the oft-repeated tale of a wind-broken horse
Costing him a windfall at the races.
As the light fades they trudge against the frigid wind
Along the windbreak to their cars
To navigate homeward along the windswept roads
Barely visible through the windshields encrusted with frost.

TOGETHER

Two together
Hands held
Stroll alone
Ignoring others
Whispering quietly
Spontaneously smiling
Laughing heartily
Love unspoken
Love entwined

LATER

Two friends
Sit together
Space shared
Hands held
Words unspoken
Private thoughts
Comfortable solitude

LISTEN

Whispers of hidden meaning
woven through his spoken words
hint at some secret message
sent with a wishful hope
the code might be broken
by someone in the circle of conversation.

Later,
in a quiet corner
off limits to the restraints of formality
I test the lock with careful, subtle questions.
With hesitation, the door to his inner conflict opens
I listen, I empathize, I respond
beyond the normal superficial human contact.

The pain in his eyes softens
One ear is not enough to drive away the pain
Perhaps, tomorrow the door will open more easily
Another person will hear the whispers
chose to go beyond the mundane
to share a quiet moment
of inner thoughts and pain
hidden behind the façade of living.

RESPITE

A quiet moment
Stolen from the busy-ness
Quietly sitting and re-ordering my thoughts
Focusing away from the frantic activity
Seeking a tranquil respite
An opportunity
To breathe deeply
To renew my energy
For the next crisis of decision
I will face today

STEPS

A thousand thousand steps
Through eons of living
Beat a path
Across the meadows
Over rocky inclines
Along meandering streams
Through scattered forests

Steps of the young
Steps of the old
Steps of the dying

Paths to adventure
Paths to new friendships
Paths to war

Tentative steps
Bold steps
Steps taken in fear

Each step followed by another

Sometimes alone
Sometimes with others

Each step disappearing in the dust of time

MOTHER

Your mother is gone from life
Never from your memory.
She gave you life.
She raised you.
She cared for and loved you.
It was not always easy between you
Your lives together became part of who you are...
A complex mix of both her and your father
Moulded together within your own personality.
She is the only mother you will ever have.
You will miss her at the most unexpected times...
In quiet moments, at family gatherings, at times of celebration
She will suddenly be there.
A thread in the fabric of your life.
Grieve for her today,
Celebrate her life tomorrow,
She lives forever within you.

MY INNER QUILT

The patterns I weave each day
Arranged together
Become the quilt of my memory.
Each square a moment in my existence
        ...moments of uncertainty
        ...moments of decisiveness
        ...moments of love
        ...moments of fear
        ...moments of peace
        ...moments of trauma
Each a part of the other
Sewn together with fine strands
Of my inner spirit
Piecing me together
Making me into a singular being.

HIJACKED

The fiery dance of the sun settling into the lake
The gurgle and swirl of water in the stream
The smooth feel of a newborn's skin
The earthy aroma of newly turned soil
The salivating taste of chocolate mousse
A quiet walk along a forest path
All conspire
To suddenly, unexpectantly highjack our senses
To a tranquil refuge.
Once there,
They calm our racing thoughts
They unwind our tightly strung emotions.
We escape from the hurriedness of our lives.

SUPERFICIAL VIEW

Soft eyes
Full lips
Delicate hands
Slim Waist
Long legs
Calm aura
No hint
To what lies within

Darting eyes
Pursed lips
Sweating hands
Thin waist
Restless legs
Uptight aura
No secret
To what lies within

THE HANDSHAKE

From out of the crowd
A hand emerges
A flash of anticipation
Which will it be?
— a water pumper —
— a produce squeezer —
— a slippery slider —
— a clammy grasper —
— a dead nothing —
— a frantic clutcher —
— an official greeter —
— a desperate clinger —
— a sincere welcome —
— a first connection —
— a potential friend —
— a secret lover —

THE JOURNEY

Where go my thoughts
In a moment of quiet stillness?
Out beyond to the unexplored
Inward to my secret self
Somewhere unexpected in the space between

Wherever the journey today,
I revel in the smoky mysteries of new possibilities
Aware of intellectual risk in the pursuits of my mind
An unknown destination of emotional response
More real than a dream

Are there places my thoughts will not go?
Walls of rationality they cannot penetrate
Seas of tangled emotion that drown them
Cultural barriers that confuse them
A sense of self not strong enough to follow them to their end

I hope not!
I want to let my thoughts wander free
Unencumbered by where I've been
Unrestrained by fear
Able to pursue every potential
Offered by unfettered freedom

YOU AND I

I feel you here within me
A part of everything I do
You share my triumphs
You feel my pain
You anticipate my thoughts
You know me better than I know myself
Together we share our lives
Each day a new beginning

A WINTER NIGHT

I feel the cold bite my cheeks
My fingers tingle
I taste the crispness of the air
The next breath sears my lungs
I hear the ice crack across the pond
The wind buffets me
I see a mirage of life through the swirling snow
I smell the bonfire smoke
I join the others around the circle of dancing light
The laughter of friendship warms us

PICTURES

The joyous moments of our lives
Caught in pictures
Fill the pages of our album
No images of sorrow
No images of pain
We share only the happy times
The sad and lonely times are locked away
In the pictures of our minds, in the memories of our heart
Too personal for public viewing

The pictures assailing us in the headlines of the day
Display all the pain, sorrow, and fear
Of the world around us
Imprinted on our minds forever
They tear at our heartstrings
They disgust us
They haunt us
A stark contrast
To the images in our album

146

UNCERTAINTY

The fog of everyday living engulfs us.
Subtle sensations of uncertainty
Emanate from our memory of unsettling experiences
Jeopardizing any thoughts of new direction.
Not enough to destroy the entirety of those possibilities
Rather creating a tentative, unsure consequence of outcome.
Enough to arrest the tenacious action needed to drive us
Towards a future devoid of past hindrance.

We wait for a strong wind of self-assurance
To lift the fog
To calm the sensations of uncertainty
To give us strength
To go beyond the dreams of possibilities
To seek them out
In the brilliance of a life
Re-born to new adventure.

SOLITARY THOUGHTS

I sit alone in a busy world
Not noticed by the rushing crowds
A solitary person with solitary thoughts
Not moved to be part of the outside world
Satisfied to dwell within
Not afraid to revel in my own whimsical meanderings

THE REFUGE

The bench beckoned to me from its secluded refuge
Hidden under the brooding branches of the stoic maple.
Carved from a single slab of granite, warmly discoloured with age
A quiet spot to rest my body weary from a long and tortuous climb

I slowly lower myself to the bench
Gripping the worn edge with my hands
The coolness and smooth contours of the stone a welcome relief
From the heat and stress of the day

I breathe in the space around me
I hear the buzz of insects, the sigh of long grasses
I smell the dark, spongy earth beneath my feet
A solitary fleeting moment of tranquility

Unwillingly, I push up from my seat
My hands reluctant to part from the bench until the last moment
I reach the path and glance quickly back
For one last wistful look at my unexpected refuge

DARK VOICES

Our dark inner voices rise unbidden from some deep lingering place
Without warning they drive away our intellectual reasoning
Needing no words to exert control
Anger misleads us
Bitterness disillusions us
Fear impales us
Unchallenged these emotions possess the power to ruin us
But for those who chose
Laughter and tears are but a breath away
To cleanse our spirits of these dark clouds

WARM WELCOME

Beyond the barrier a delicious young woman waves excitedly
Her exuberance bouncing her into the air
A warm welcome awaits someone in the pressing crowd behind me
I glance around to spot the lucky traveller
No set of eyes is riveted in her direction
Only brief smiles as others spot her in the crowd

I speculate

He must still be inside
Impatiently held back by customs formalities
Anxious to be in the arms of his lover
Too long separated
Only moments away from infectious joy

I could hurry away, there is no need to linger
Rather I stop and step to the side
Waiting to see him burst into her arms
Wanting to vicariously relive such love
A reminder of my past when I was greeted in such a way

Her waves become a clapping of excitement
I see no handsome youth
Only a shuffling old man approaching
She envelops him in a hug so huge he disappears
"Gramps, you're here, I've missed you"

He has lived well
To be greeted by such a radiance of love
I turn and walk away
A smile on my face
A tear in my eye

REST AWHILE

A soft evening breeze brushes past me.
The Muskoka chair a welcome spot to rest awhile.
Gentle waves caress the sandy shore
in a rhythmic beat of soothing sound.
Quiet tranquility settles around me with a sigh of comfort.

Through the vapour of weariness my roving eye
settles on a man and woman
framed by the sunset at the water's edge.
Their figures silhouetted in a fiery aura
of togetherness.

As the last vestiges of sunlight disappear
I drift away to the place of nothingness.
The sounds and sights now merely background music
to the wanderings of my dreams.

VOICES

Each day a multitude of voices clamour for our attention
Their messages unheard above the clatter
We are:
>   too concerned for self to heed a trembling call for help
>   too unsure to accept a quiet word of praise
>   too afraid to confront an unreasoned burst of anger
>   too busy to hear a friend's tearful tale

It takes time to separate the voices from the fray
Each day, we can with perseverance:
>   hear the voice most in need —act upon their word
>   acknowledge the kind words —let them warm our heart
>   address the words of anger —before they turn to rage
>   seek out the friend —be the sympathetic ear

Listen carefully!
For those of us who choose
the words and feelings important to the symphony of our lives
will rise above the babble.

ALONE

I walk alone
along a mindless path.
My thoughts scurrying elsewhere
flitting from track to track
immune to the sights and sounds around me.

I pause to rest
weary from the walking mental jumbo.
Something pecks at my insular thoughts.
The songs of morning birds sneak through.
I search the branches for a glimpse.

I breathe deeply and move on
connected now to the path I walk.
No longer alone!

TWO PERSONS

Two persons
Joined by the harmony of love.
So close their thoughts eerily coincide
Their divergent views heard without words.
Their moods intertwined
Basking in the essence of each other
Relishing the nuances of anticipation.
Confident to allow each a space apart
To breathe a breath of self
To keep from drowning in a suffocating sea of togetherness.

SEARCHING

A gentle touch
An unexpected whispered word
A glance beyond the norm
Messages of yearning
Between two in this vast room
Each unknown to the other
Brought together by chance
Hoping for a spark of connection
Ready for more than they've known till now

WARMTH

I drift
Allowing my mind's eye to look from beyond
Skirting the edges of reality
Able to see the fringes of shimmering energy surrounding me
Each breath drawing the life force from each part of me
   …integrating it
   …swimming in it
   …freeing it.
An envelope of warmth around my space.

LEADERSHIP

Progress has been slow
Too little leadership
Too busy with more important things
Now, He demands to meet those responsible
Septic words of criticism spew forth
No restraint
No concern for impact
A venting of pent-up anger and selfishness
Targeted at those too junior to respond
All hope of success evaporates
Into a vacuum of ill will.

RHAPSODY OF WAR

The rhapsody of war builds to a crescendo
Planes far overhead birth their missiles of death
Bombs explode their terror in a blinding flash
Tanks spit snarling shells of destruction
The technology of war wreaks its' havoc.

Men and women advance across the sands
Skirmish through the streets
Hunting those who oppose them.
Shots ricochet off walls,
Thud into bodies.
No distinction for friend or foe.

Mothers weep
Comrades cry for those who die
Children ask why?

DARKNESS

At night,
Too many corners of the world
Are crowded by cowering children
Afraid of the light of day

Too many horrors have been seen
Alone, hungry, despairing
They would rather stay hidden forever.
The darkness of their world obscured
By the darkness of the night

THOUGHTS

Thoughts appear and disappear
Racing like a shooting star
Across the firmament of our intellectual pursuits

Some are bright and shine with insight
Intriguing enough to dwell upon
Others are but a faint glow
Easily forgotten in the rush of time

At times, snippets of incomplete sightings confuse
Not enough to fully perceive their meaning
Their context seems obscure

Not yet mature!
A part of some bigger whole
To later delight us in its brilliance
As it burns across the panorama of our thoughts

ALONE

She wakes one day

The light is gone!

She has drifted into a fog
It feels close, almost suffocating
No guideposts can be seen or felt

She is drowning in a sea of mist
Every breath takes her deeper
Into the dark place within herself

Isolated from friends and family
Unable to cry for help
Her silent anguish goes unheard

She is alone!

Deeper and deeper she spirals
There is no light in this place
—— only darkness ——

Without help, there will be no awakening!

INTERLUDE

Conjured by the flowering flames
Mystical meanderings warm my mind.
Transporting me to whimsical places
Alive with their own sounds and smells.
No thought for consequence of outcome
A place to rest awhile.

156

SECURE

Awaken your senses to the unexpected
Revel in the subtleties of the mundane
Find comfort in the simplicity of the moment

Hear the whispered songs playing in the wind
See the shimmering images dancing in the setting sun
Smell the earthy fragrances swirling after the warm spring rain
Touch the wee fingers exploring your face

No need to search further for tranquility
Experience the pleasure of being
Secure to breathe in the life around you

MARRIAGE

Two strangers
Love found us.
It crept up and stole our hearts
We now share our lives, our hopes, our dreams
Together we are one
Apart we yearn each for the other.
Our love, tentative at first,
led us to this day.
The day of our marriage
    - a day to declare our love before family and friends
    - a day to celebrate our commitment
    - a day to remember the rest of our lives

We rejoice to have found each other.

Printed in the United States
by Baker & Taylor Publisher Services